PROSPECT PARK

PROSPECT PARK

OLMSTED & VAUX'S

Brooklyn Masterpiece

To Richard
Enjoy The Prospect
Pert A Place
David P. Colley
Mark Colley

David P. Colley

PHOTOGRAPHS BY

Elizabeth Keegin Colley

IN COLLABORATION WITH THE PROSPECT PARK ALLIANCE

PRINCETON ARCHITECTURAL PRESS

NEW YORK

Published by
Princeton Architectural Press
37 East 7th Street
New York, New York 10003
Visit our website at www.papress.com

Printed and bound in China by C&C Joint Printing Co., (Guangdong) Ltd.
16 15 14 13 4 3 2 1 First edition

This publication was made possible with the help of a grant by
Furthermore: a program of the J. M. Kaplan Fund.

Editors: Nicola Bednarek Brower and Jacob Moore
Designers: Paul Wagner and Elana Schlenker

Special thanks to: Meredith Baber, Sara Bader, Janet Behning, Fannie Bushin,
Megan Carey, Carina Cha, Andrea Chlad, Benjamin English, Russell Fernandez, Will Foster,
Jan Hartman, Jan Haux, Diane Levinson, Jennifer Lippert, Katharine Myers,
Margaret Rogalski, Dan Simon, Andrew Stepanian, Sara Stemen, and Joseph Weston of
Princeton Architectural Press —Kevin C. Lippert, publisher

Library of Congress Cataloging-in-Publication Data
Colley, David.
Prospect Park : Olmsted and Vaux's Brooklyn masterpiece /
David P. Colley ; photography by Elizabeth Keegin Colley. — First edition.
pages cm
ISBN 978-1-61689-118-3 (hardback)
1. Prospect Park (New York, N.Y.) I. Title.
F128.65.P76C65 2013
974.7'23—dc23   2012034280

Contents

Foreword

I DIDN'T GROW UP IN PROSPECT PARK. MY NEIGHBORHOOD park was Riverside, and Central Park was where I sometimes went on weekends as a child. Prospect Park was, to me, a mythical land in distant Brooklyn, across the East River and reachable only by a long trip on the subway. Later, when I was hired as a member of the first corps of urban-park rangers in 1979 (assigned to Central Park), I first started to explore Prospect Park. Conducting research for tours of Central Park, I learned that the Brooklyn park was also the work of Frederick Law Olmsted and Calvert Vaux, the celebrated designers of Central, Riverside, and Morningside Parks as well as many other great urban parks across the country.

As we worked on our tours and traded bits of knowledge, my Brooklyn colleagues supplied the first lesson on Prospect Park: "Olmsted and Vaux designed Central Park, learned from their mistakes, and then designed Prospect Park." That claim seemed to be an audacious bit of Brooklyn boosterism, anticipating the unabashed cheerleading of its eventual borough president, Marty Markowitz. After all, everyone knew that Central Park was the greatest park in the world; how could it be challenged by its smaller and younger sibling?

Gradually I came to know Prospect Park myself, first while working for the urban-park rangers when Mayor Ed Koch and Park Commissioner Gordon Davis appointed Tupper Thomas the park's first administrator. (Shortly thereafter, Thomas worked to establish the Prospect Park Alliance, a sister organization to the Central Park Conservancy.) Later, while running the natural resources and horticulture divisions of the parks department, I came to know the foresters and horticulturists working to restore Prospect Park's landscape and care for its towering trees. While overseeing the art and antiquities division, I participated in the restoration of the park's stunning public sculptures, an outdoor museum of nineteenth-and early twentieth-century bronzes, including Frederick MacMonnies's magnificent, muscular *Horse Tamers* and the neo-classical splendor of the Soldiers and Sailors Memorial Arch at Grand Army Plaza.

It wasn't until I was appointed parks commissioner in 2002 by Mayor Michael Bloomberg that I was able to devote my attention to the entire park and came to understand its many virtues as a living and historic landscape, as a sports and culture mecca for the marvelously diverse residents of Brooklyn, as the borough's most important and enduring park, and perhaps as the most perfectly realized landscape design of Olmsted and Vaux.

In the intervening twenty-three years, from when I started as a park ranger to my appointment as parks commissioner, Prospect Park and its surroundings, indeed all of Brooklyn, had seen unparalleled growth, restoration, and improvement. The Prospect Park Alliance, led by a hardworking and dedicated volunteer board, and the careful and inclusive nurturing of elected officials and community organizations by Thomas, who served for three decades as its ebullient and unsinkable administrator and president, had brought the park back from the precipice of decay to a glorious state of rebirth. The Long Meadow and the Ravine woodlands had undergone a careful, decades-long restoration. The Picnic House, Tennis House, and Boathouse had all been rebuilt and reactivated, the latter now serving as the nation's first urban Audubon Center. Outside of Prospect Park proper, the Parade Ground, which spawned so many baseball legends, had been reimagined as a state-of-the-art athletic complex. The park's cultural neighbors, the Brooklyn Botanic Garden, the Brooklyn Museum, and the Brooklyn Public Library, shared and strengthened the park's rebirth with their own massive restoration and expansion programs.

This was the Prospect Park I encountered and explored; as I soon discovered, it had indeed some aspects that could not be found in its sibling parks. Central Park, perfect as it is, is a long and narrow rectangle, surrounded by tall buildings. Despite the designers' exacting efforts to create escapes from city streets in winding paths, bucolic woodlands, and artistic reinterpretations of English landscape gardens and of the precipices and cloves of the Catskills, as a visitor you are always conscious of the city around you. During Prospect Park's development, the real estate pressures were fewer, and the park was designed in the form of a large, rambunctious, bulging diamond. There are currently only a few tall apartment buildings along the park's perimeter. Standing in the middle of Prospect Park, on the Long Meadow or Nethermead, or deep in the wooded Ravine, you truly feel as if you were in a vast English landscape designed by Capability Brown or in a deep woodland in the Adirondack Mountains.

Prospect Park shares Central Park's three major landscape features—meadow, lake, and woodland—as well as a winding carriage drive. But its Long Meadow undulates for a mile, much longer than any of the meadows of its older sibling. The Lake is bigger than Central Park's Lake, its intimate backwaters more secluded, its vast expanse almost an inland sea. And its Woodland and Ravine are deeper, darker, and more mysterious than its cousins in Central Park, the Ramble and North Woods. To stand in the Long Meadow amid its rolling hills and not to see its terminus, or to stroll under the gloomy beauty of the stone arch in the Ravine and not to sense the city around you, is to feel in your heart and soul the essence of the romantic landscape, which reaches its apotheosis in Prospect Park.

Prospect Park also plays a role different from that of Central Park, which is in some ways the world's park, but not necessarily the signature park of Manhattan, which also has Riverside Park, the large landscaped parks of Harlem and Washington Heights, the historic squares of Lower Manhattan, and the new West Side waterfront parks. Brooklyn has Marine Park, its largest park, way out on its southern fringe, the Works Progress Administration–era recreational hub of McCarren Park on its northwest corner, and the new Brooklyn Bridge Park next to Brooklyn Heights. But Prospect Park is definitely Brooklyn's park, its heart, its centerpiece, and a magnet for all of Brooklyn to come out and enjoy sports, music, history, and plants and animals, but most of all to leave behind the busy streets and re-create oneself in the perfection of nature tamed and reimagined, perfected and yet still wild—a modern paradise free and open to all.

Adrian Benepe
New York City Parks Commissioner

Strolling across the Long Meadow
on a summer's day is one
of the great pleasures of living
in Brooklyn.

Acknowledgments

WE HAVE HAD THE GOOD FORTUNE TO SPEND THE LAST FIVE years surrounded by the beauty of Prospect Park and immersed in its magnificent history. We want to thank the Prospect Park Alliance and Furthermore, a J. M. Kaplan Fund program, for their support in writing this book, and Tupper Thomas for her extensive knowledge of this and other urban parks and for her infectious enthusiasm and gracious hospitality. We appreciate the analysis of former Alliance chairman Henry Christensen III and thank all the park's current and former staff, especially Eugene Patron, who managed the manuscript early on; Christian Zimmerman for interpreting Olmsted and Vaux; Anne Wong for introducing us to the park's trees and understory; archivist Amy Peck for retrieving material and for her suggestions; Barbara McTiernan for the park's recent history; and Pam Fishman and Maria Cobo for explaining educational outreach. Thanks to Lucio Schiavone, Carousel operator for background information; architect Ralph Carmosino for detailing the Boathouse restoration; Ed Toth for his expertise on native plants; Gabriel Willow for sharing his encyclopedic wildlife knowledge; Glen Gunzer for explaining the drainage system; Mary Fox Zimmerman and Dennis Madge for Ravine restoration history; Eric Landau for Com Com background; Felicity Frisbie for design insights; and Chris Werben for his efforts in the final days. We also thank Stanton Wood, Brenda Corbin, Robyn Bellamy, Alden Maddry, James Snow, Karen LeRiche, Margaret Ring, Josephine Pittari, P. J. Greiner, Carol Anastasio, Crystal Gaudio, Elyse Newman, Louise Smith, Scott Morris, and Prospect Park Zoo's Debbie Dieneman Keim and Harvey Seiderbaum.

We appreciate the time given us by former New York mayor Ed Koch, former Brooklyn borough president Howard Golden, his assistant Marylyn Gelber, and the current borough president, Marty Markowitz. Thanks to the New York City Parks Department, former commissioners Adrian Benepe and Gordon Davis, staff members

Jonathan Kuhn and Kaitlin Griffen, former Brooklyn commissioner Julius Spiegel, current commissioner Kevin Jeffrey, and Chief of Staff Martin Maher. Park volunteers who assisted included William Novak, the late Robert Makla, the late Richard Engquist and Jane Brody, and former curators Joseph and Mary Mertz and Donald Simon, as well as FIDO members Charlotte Gemmel and Tony Chiappelloni.

Catherine Nagel of the City Parks Alliance offered perspective on the park movement, as did Alex Garvin; authors Charles Beveridge and Francis Kowsky gave insight into Olmsted and Vaux. Hofstra professor Brett Bennington examined glaciers, Horace Morancie introduced us to the Drummer's Grove, and Jack Walsh to Celebrate Brooklyn! and youthful days in the park. Paul Keim of the Brooklyn Bird Club enlightened us about bats, birds, and insects. Other birders were Peter Dorash, Eric Slayton, Carole Mebus, Francie Von Mertens, and Anne Hogenboom. Kimberly Maier, of the Old Stone House of Brooklyn, dissected the Battle of Brooklyn, along with Hunter College Professor William J. Parry.

Additional individuals who helped include: Mike Armstrong, *Phoenix*'s former editor; Russell Flinchum of the Century Association; Jeff Richman of Green-Wood Cemetery; Agnes Keating of the Newport Polo Club; Sally Williams and Rinna Ibraham of the Brooklyn Museum; Horace Laffaye; Stan Portnoy; Alan Goldberg; Mary McCormick; Pierre Dillard; Sproule Love; the late Marjorie Parker Smith; Dr. Murray Glickman; Al Franquinha; Francis Marone; and Walker Blankinship. We thank all the people we met in the park by chance, chatted with, and photographed.

Librarians were invaluable: Diane Shaw, archivist at the Lafayette College Library; the staff of the New York Public Library rare books room; Leonora A. Gidlund, director of the New York City Municipal Archives; Janet Parks, a curator; Shelley Hayreh, archivist at Columbia University, and Don Shumaker, curator at the Mack Trucks Historical Museum. Local libraries contributed: the Brooklyn Public Library (Joy Holland); the Brooklyn Historical Society; and the libraries in Bridgehampton, New York, and Bethlehem and Easton, Pennsylvania.

We appreciate photography help: Joan and Albert Kronick, for their interview and use of their terrace to photograph the park from on high; Ramon Bryant and Procida Realty for access to the rooftop of the Richard Meier building; Luis Lemus for carefully lifting us up in the bucket truck; Bill, Peggy, Sparkie, Bill, and Bonnie of Fisk's Camera Shop, who have always kept our equipment going; and John Kish IV, a great friend and fine photographer, who solved technology glitches.

We are indebted to our editors, Nicola Bednarek Brower and Jacob Moore, for their considerable time and ideas, and designers Paul Wagner and Elana Schlenker for their handsome layout. Friends and our extended family provided support—Ian and Helen Ann Hetherington, Stafford and Susan Keegin—but we especially thank our immediate family for establishing what is really important in life: Padraic, Erin, and little Leah; Chris and Zhao Ya; and Tim, our black lab, whose spontaneous exuberance upon entering the park was matched only by our own.

We thank you all.

Park Distances

Park Perimeter (outside sidewalks)	3.75 mi.
Park Drives Running Lane (inside Park)	3.35 mi.
Grand Army to Center Dr (& West Dr)	1.16 mi.
Length of Center Drive	.57 mi.
Center Dr (& West Dr) to Wellhouse Dr	.23 mi.
Length of Wellhouse Drive	.62 mi.
Wellhouse Dr (& West Dr) to Wellhouse Dr (& East Dr), around Lake	1.14 mi.
Wellhouse (& East Dr) to Center Dr	.12 mi.
Center Dr (& East Dr) to Grand Army	.77 mi.

8 T H   A V

WINDSOR PL.

16TH ST.

15TH ST.

14TH ST.

13TH ST.

PROSPECT AVENUE

HOWARD PL.

FULLER PL.

10TH AVE.

16TH ST.

SHERMAN ST.

11TH AVE.

BARTEL-PRITCHARD CIRCLE

Acanthus Columns
No vehicles

F, G M 15th St.-Prospect Park

PROSPECT PARK SOUTHWEST

WEST DRIVE

1

7

Friends or Quaker Cemetery (Private)

20TH ST.

19TH ST.

PROSPECT EXPRESSWAY

PROSPECT AVENUE

TERRACE PL.

SEELEY ST.

TEMPLE

VANDERBILT ST.

E. 7TH ST.

REEVE PL.

F, G M Ft. Hamilton Pkwy.

SHERMAN ST.

GREENWOOD AVE.

PROSPECT PARK SOUTHWEST

CE

Vanderbilt St. Playground

LOOKOUT HILL

Wellhouse

Maryland Monument

Turkey Oak

WELLHOUSE DRIVE

WEST DRIVE

Rustic Shelter

PENINSULA

Terrace Bridge

Willow Oak

FT. HAMILTON PKWAY

LAKE

WEST ISLAND

THREE ISLANDS

PARK CIRCLE

Horse Tamers

CATON PL.

CONEY ISLAND AVE.

EAST DRIVE

Police Annex and Park Field House

Prospect Park Tennis Center

1

2

PARADE

3

GROUND

7

8

9

10

11

STRATFORD RD.

WESTMINSTER RD.

ARGYLE RD.

CATON AVE.

CHURCH AVE.

RUGBY RD.

MARLBOROUGH RD.

E. 16TH ST.

Rustic Shelter

The Peristyle

Rustic Shelter

DUCK ISLAND

Rustic Shelter

4

6

5

PARKSIDE AVENUE

PARADE PL.

CROOKE AVE.

ST. PAUL'S PL.

WOODRUFF AVE.

Playground

The Perg

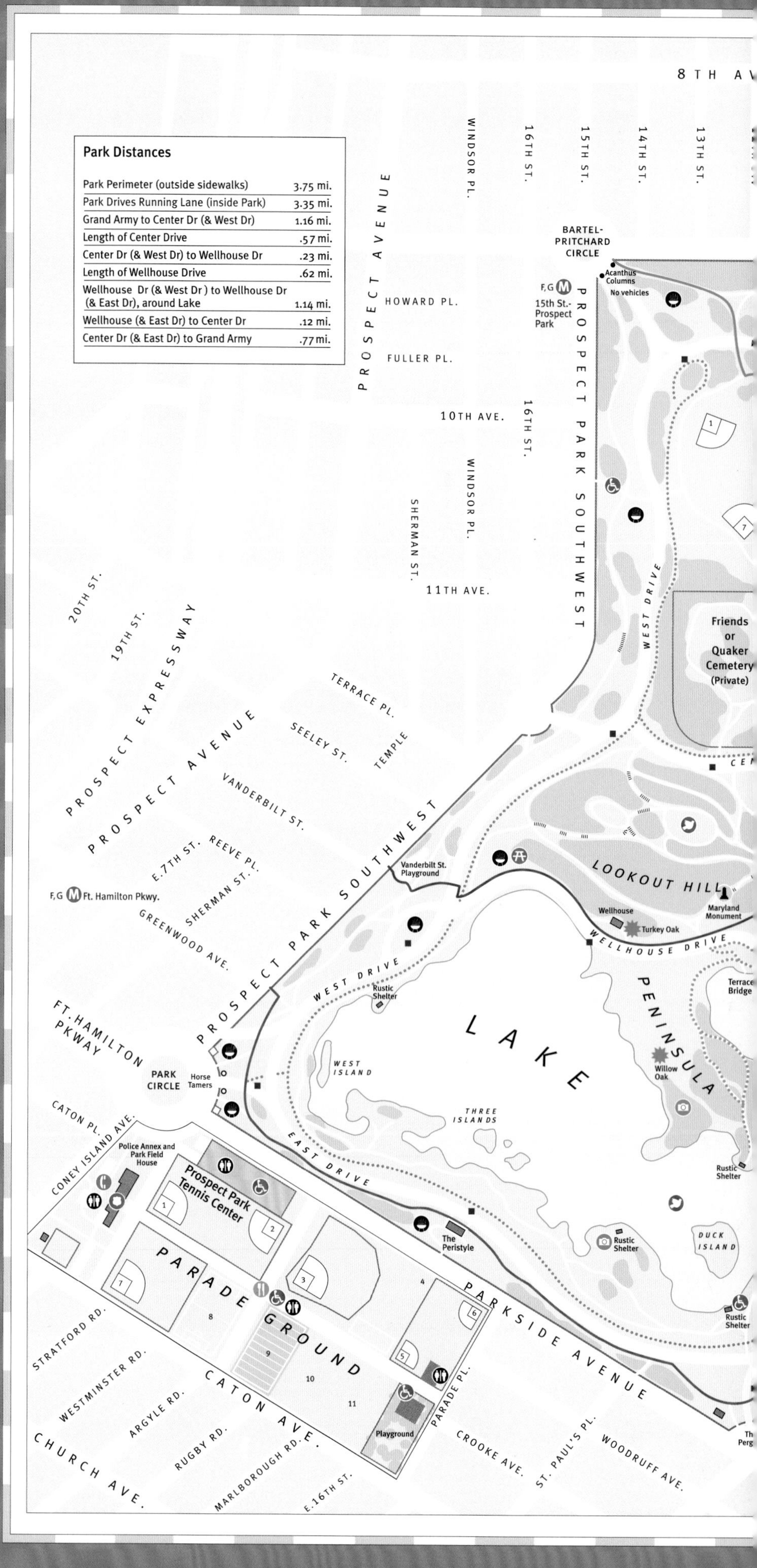

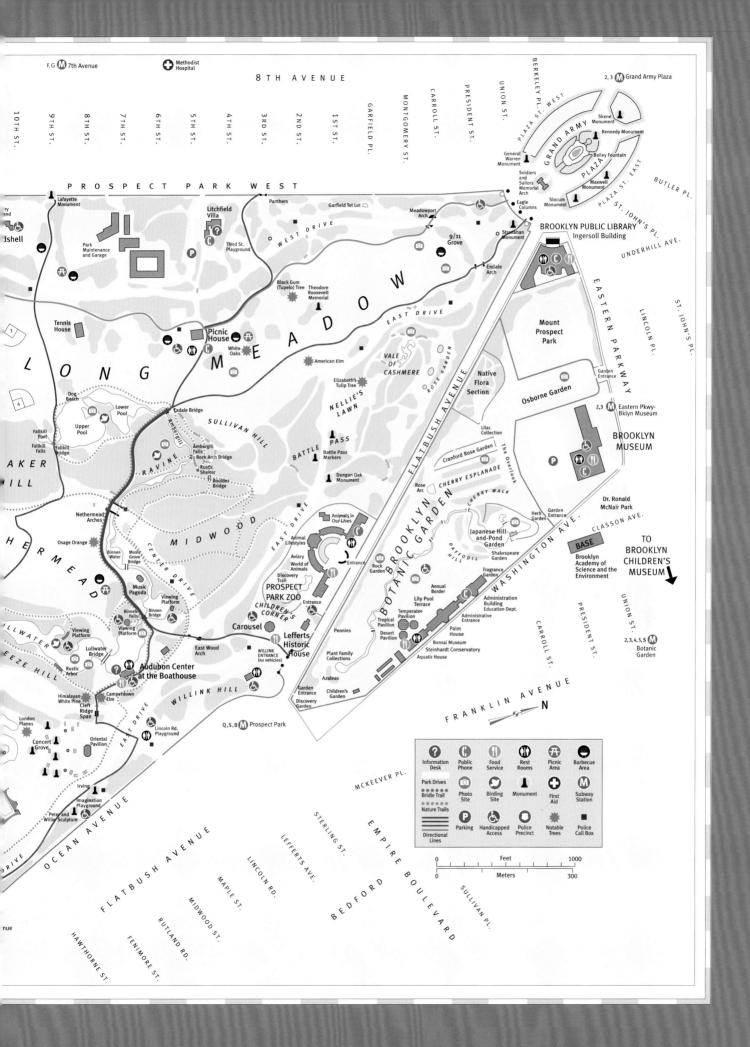

Introduction

A male northern shoveler
between two mallards on the
shore of the Lake

IT HAS BEEN CALLED MAGNIFICENT, EVEN PERFECT; FROM the beginning Prospect Park has been described in superlatives. Designers Frederick Law Olmsted and Calvert Vaux considered it a work of art and their masterpiece, superior even to their Central Park, the gold standard of American pleasure grounds.[1] Nineteenth-century New York diarist George Templeton Strong reluctantly agreed that the celebrated Central Park had been matched and might even have been outdone.[2] Today Prospect Park remains all that it was intended to be: an exquisite public space that provides a rural refuge in the heart of sprawling and boisterous Brooklyn.

Within its bucolic 585 acres one is transported from the chaos and clamor of urban life to an idyllic and tranquil realm of graceful meadows, dense forests, and placid lake waters that glitter with the changing light of day and where egrets, ducks, and gulls inhabit beguiling little isles and an intricate shoreline. Prospect Park is as much illusion as it is reality. Olmsted and Vaux understood that the natural world seldom displays itself in the ideal, and they set out to construct an impression of nature at its most harmonious and sublime. They used the elements of meadow, woods, and water and designed them to be appreciated not only for their own individual beauty but also for their combined effect in creating a wondrous landscape.

But there was a greater purpose in Prospect Park than embellishing nature, one that is as relevant today as it was in 1866 when ground was broken. Brooklyn was expanding exponentially throughout the nineteenth century, from a community of 5,740 people in 1800 to a borough of 1,166,582 by the century's end. As Brooklyn grew, immigrants from abroad and migrants from the American hinterlands filled its streets and occupied tenements, where many lived in squalor, plagued by disease and without any connection to nature. Prospect Park would be a place where everyone could enjoy nature's calming, cleansing effects and be exposed to uncontaminated air.

PROSPECT PARK

Here Brooklynites could lie on the grass, walk through a forest streaked with sunbeams, or dangle a limb over the side of a boat on the Lake. They could shed their worries, if only momentarily, and experience what Olmsted called "enlarged freedom."[3] In addition, the park would attract affluent new residents to expand Brooklyn's material wealth and elevate its stature.

Prospect Park realized its designers' vision of the democratic ideal where people would mingle and socialize openly—and without reservation—with others from diverse backgrounds, cultures, and socioeconomic levels. The day laborer would rub shoulders with the millionaire, and American democracy would be the better for it. What was true about the beauty and purpose of the park in the nineteenth century is still true: it is a sanctuary that also fulfills its role as a melting pot.

Imagine for a moment a visitor from the nineteenth century returning to the park today. Undoubtedly, he would be overwhelmed by the changes in Brooklyn, by the expanse of the borough, by the towering, distant, and jagged Manhattan skyline, and by the swirling, often deafening noise from the strange contraptions called automobiles that career around Grand Army Plaza. But after the initial shock, he would be delighted and amazed to find that much of Prospect Park remains fundamentally unchanged.

For a visitor entering through the dark tunnel of Endale Arch, the first exposure to the park is a bright view of the sunlit Long Meadow.

PROSPECT PARK

Aerial view of Prospect Park, 2008

Until the 1890s, Grand Army Plaza, the main entrance to Prospect Park known then simply as "the Plaza," was a flat expanse interrupted only by a lonely statue of President Abraham Lincoln and a domed fountain. It was hot and dry in summer and windswept in winter, and the loudest sounds came from horse-drawn wagons, whose iron wheels rumbled and banged across the cobbled streets, and from the screeching and scraping of trolley cars. Standing in the Plaza today, our visitor finds himself surrounded by a looming cityscape and dwarfed by the massive Soldiers and Sailors Memorial Arch. As he makes his way to the park, he sees that the entrance is now elaborately delineated with marble columns and balustrades, which were absent during his day. He passes the statue of James S. T. Stranahan, the park's founder and a familiar figure in late nineteenth-century Brooklyn, still on its pedestal where it was dedicated in 1891. Our visitor moves deeper into the park, onto a winding path framed by varieties of shrubs and by towering trees whose leaves and branches shade the walkway. The tumult of the city begins to recede as he approaches Endale Arch, one of five grotto-like entrances that penetrate the twenty-foot-high berm that surrounds much of the park, hides the city, and silences the urban din. He makes his way through the small tunnel onto the threshold of the Long Meadow and is greeted by a very familiar view—of a sunlit Eden that is green, lush, rolling, meandering, and filled with people playing, chatting, walking, and dozing.

The city fades, as he walks down the great curving lawn and through dappled sunlight, past a singular majestic American elm and stands of oaks that cast long, sliverlike shadows on the green. He passes the rugged and dark forested Ravine, where he recalls the winding pathways, rippling streams, refreshing pools, and cascading waterfalls. He enters the woods that are nearly unchanged, except

that the trees are taller and the understory is more dense. The Nethermead also remains remarkably familiar to our visitor and he walks across this expansive clearing to the Lullwater, bordered now at its headwaters by an elegant boathouse. He passes through the Cleft Ridge Span, whose archway frames the Oriental Pavilion, and on to the Concert Grove. Sadly, the Concert Grove House of his day is gone but he sees the same sweeping Lake panorama of 120 years ago. The Carriage Concourse was removed, but in its place is Lakeside—including two ice rinks, a cafe, and public spaces overlooking the Lake— a testament to the park's achievement of meeting modern needs with green design. Ford Pond is gone, but the Lake is essentially as it was a century ago. Fishermen dot the shore, waterfowl move in clusters, and an occasional rustic shelter is still visible.

Our visitor is delighted to see the excursion boat, *Independence*, silently gliding by, carrying visitors around the Lake. Olmsted championed the electrically powered boat, and a replica still begins its tour at the Boathouse and travels down the serpentine Lullwater, which is filled with turtles, dragonflies, swans, and black-crowned night herons, and then on to the Lake, weaving around the islands. In this setting it is easy for the passengers to forget that Prospect Park is in the heart of the most densely populated city in the United States.

Essentially, the experience of the park is the same for our visitor as it would have been more than a century ago. There are new structures and paved carriageways that are filled with joggers and cyclists, but the basic landscape—the good bones—remains, and the park's population is still a mixture of immigrants. Instead of the newly

ABOVE
Olmsted and Vaux had
a vision for a natural haven
and gathering place for the people
of Brooklyn. The Long Meadow
continues to meet that vision in
the twenty-first century.

RIGHT
An exuberant unicyclist scoots
by the Long Meadow.

arrived English, Irish, and Germans of the mid- to late nineteenth century, today's Americans are richly diverse and come from all over the world—from Bangladeshis and Haitians to women wrapped head to toe in burquas, from men in yarmulkes to African drummers, from Chinese brides posing for photographs by the Lullwater and the Lake to Peruvians flying their kites on the Long Meadow. All are there to picnic, relax, bicycle, play baseball, go horseback riding, or enjoy one of the numerous new activities and programs available.

While the croquet players, archers, and tennis players who crowded the meadows in the late nineteenth century are gone, tennis is still very popular, though no longer played on the three hundred grass courts that once graced the Long Meadow and the Nethermead, but rather on well-maintained courts at the Tennis Center on the edge of the Parade Ground to the south of the park. Besides sports, music plays a large role in today's park, with performances by the New York Philharmonic, the Metropolitan Opera, and musicians in Celebrate Brooklyn! events. And knowledge of the environment is emphasized as small children flock to the Audubon Center at the Boathouse to learn the difference between a dragonfly and a damselfly.

Throughout the 150 years since its inception, Prospect Park has weathered political and economic storms and accommodated change while maintaining its essential character. From the beginning and during critical times, the individuals and teams involved had the energy and leadership to overcome the serious challenges that threatened the park's future. For the last thirty years, the role of stewardship has been assumed by a public-private partnership between the City of New York and the Prospect Park Alliance, which sustains the park on a myriad of levels—from maintenance, security, and the restoration of landscape and buildings to the development of environmental and educational programs. How is it that Prospect Park still so comfortably meets the needs of the modern world? What is its history? And how will it be sustained in the future? That is the story this book will tell.

Chapter One

IN THE BEGINNING

GLACIERS ONCE COVERED MUCH OF THE AREA that Prospect Park now occupies. One hundred thousand years ago, millions of tons of ice, stacked as high as one thousand feet, scoured the land that today makes up the Long Meadow and the Nethermead. The towering Labrador lobe of the Laurentide ice sheet formed the steep hills of the park's Battle Pass and the Ravine, both extensions of the Harbor Hill Moraine, a series of ridges stretching across Long Island.

The large and small boulders (erratics and cobbles, respectively) found in Prospect Park—and used to build the Boulder Bridge in the forested Midwood and the Fallkill and Ambergill waterfalls in the Ravine—were originally a part of the canyon walls of the New Jersey Palisades before they were gouged out by lumbering ice flows and deposited in the park site. The smooth outwash plain of sand and gravel that underlies Brooklyn from the Flatbush area to Coney Island came from glacial meltwater.

No one knows how many eons passed after the ice age before man appeared here. Native people inhabited the region for at least nine thousand years, living off the land and the fruits of the sea. The ground that became Prospect Park was covered with dense forest and crisscrossed by footpaths, which later became the well-traveled highways and city streets of today, including Flatbush Avenue and Kings Highway. The park's East Drive partly follows an old Native American trail that branched off of a larger path that ran between what is now Atlantic and Flatbush Avenues.

The first Europeans arrived in 1524, when the Italian explorer Giovanni da Verrazano sailed into New York Harbor. At the time Brooklyn was a collection of Lenape settlements—the Lenapes were the predominate tribe in the region—in Gowanus, Sheepshead Bay, the Flatlands, and Canarsie. The English navigator and explorer Henry Hudson, looking for a western route to Asia in 1609 for the Dutch East India Company, anchored his ship, the *Half Moon*, in Gravesend Bay. The Dutch were the first Europeans to colonize Brooklyn—which they spelled *Breukelen*—as early as 1624. An English Anabaptist community called Gravesend was chartered by the Dutch in 1645. Other Dutch groups later settled in New Amersfoort (now the Flatlands) in 1647, Midwout (Flatbush) in 1652, New Utrecht in 1657, and Boswijck (Bushwick) in 1661. The British arrived in 1664 and easily took control of New Amsterdam, which they renamed New York, and Brooklyn, ruling the area until the end of the American Revolution.

The Revolution and the Park

War came to Brooklyn in August 1776, seven weeks after the July 4 signing of the Declaration of Independence. The conflict's legacy would have a significant influence on the development of Prospect Park, as the war would give rise to the establishment of government

PREVIOUS
Spanning a segment of the bridle path, Boulder Bridge is constructed completely from ice-age erratics.

28   PROSPECT PARK

commissions—including a park commission—that carried independent and wide control. The land that became the park was an important battleground. It is in today's Prospect Park that we find the only urban Revolutionary War battle site that still exists almost as it was in 1776.

The colonists had already been rebelling against control by the Crown for a year when the British arrived in New York Harbor from Boston with an immense flotilla of four hundred ships and thousands of Redcoat soldiers and Hessian mercenaries. Under the command of General William Howe, they set up camp on Staten Island and landed a few days later in Brooklyn, where they advanced inland and collided—in what is now Prospect Park—with a small, untested force of Americans under General John Sullivan. The British had the advantage not only because of their much larger and more highly trained force but also because many of the commanders knew the lay of the land. For years the Crown had maintained its headquarters, as well as a large military presence, on Governors Island in New York Harbor and had made detailed maps of Brooklyn and Manhattan. Additionally, many of the British officers had served in colonial New York, whereas General George Washington and his commanders were strangers to the area.

Howe's strategic objectives were to capture New York—enlisting up to thirty thousand troops—to destroy the soldiers of Washington's Continental Army entrenched in what is today's Manhattan, and to take control of the Hudson River and the territory extending to Canada. The goal was to isolate New England from the rest of the colonies and hopefully end the war. Brooklyn offered a secure base for the operation as well as an abundance of provisions that could sustain the troops for years.

Washington moved his army from Boston to New York in the summer of 1776 and sent ten thousand men to Brooklyn, where he expected a British advance against his right wing. He ordered Sullivan to hold the ridgeline that extends from today's Green-Wood Cemetery to Prospect Park and the adjacent Mount Prospect Park. Instead, General Henry Clinton, Howe's field commander, struck the American left flank at Jamaica Pass, northeast of the park. A small detachment of Redcoats, under General James Grant, remained around the village of Flatbush to attack Sullivan's troops at Battle Pass, known then as Flatbush or Valley Grove Pass, which runs between a cluster of rugged hills where today joggers strain up the park's East Drive.

The Americans were arrayed in defensive positions on and around the park's Redoubt Hill, but they also launched raids against the Hessian encampment at Flatbush. The British attack came on August 27, a day that was remembered by Femmetie Hegeman Lefferts, a member of a prominent local family, as "one of the loveliest we had had that summer, the sky was so clear and bright that you could scarcely think of it as a day which was to bring so much sorrow."[1]

The Americans attempted to slow the enemy by felling the towering Dongan oak, planted in 1686 to mark the line between the squabbling villages of Flatbush and Brooklyn. It crashed to the ground at the base of Redoubt Hill and lay across Battle Pass, but it did not stop the Hessians—ordered forward and marching to the beat of drummers and fifers. Near the crest the mercenaries lowered their bayonets and charged the last few yards as British troops swept in behind the Americans from the grounds now known as the Vale of Cashmere and Nellie's Lawn, dispersing the colonials, who fled in panic across today's Long Meadow.

The meadow was bisected by country lanes and consisted of ground so swampy that the British cavalry was hesitant to cross it on horseback. "At about 9 o'clock the Rebels gave way very fast and in their retreat, across marsh and mill dam," wrote Captain Archibald Robertson of the Royal Engineers.[2] The mopping up was left to the Hessian foot soldiers, who formed circles around their enemy and bayoneted hapless Continental soldiers. Many captured Americans were undoubtedly placed on the notorious English prison ships in Wallabout Bay, Brooklyn, only to die of starvation and disease. The bones of some ten thousand prisoners who died on the ships

Battle Pass, 1866. The hills of Battle Pass were incorporated into the park's design.

were later interred at Brooklyn's Fort Greene Park, where a memorial by the firm McKim, Mead & White was erected in their honor.

Ninety years later, when Prospect Park was built, remains of many of the soldiers whose bodies had been left behind were uncovered, and the fortifications and gun pits were still evident on Redoubt Hill. The battlefield was altered slightly during the park's construction when workers removed a large knoll just behind the hill to use as fill dirt. Plans to turn it into a memorial and historical site were promoted first by Frederick Law Olmsted and Calvert Vaux—and by others through-out the years—and may someday come to fruition.[3] Three bronze plaques along East Drive mark the site: one describing the events of that day, one indicating the American line of defense, and the third, at the base of Redoubt Hill, at the spot where the Dongan oak fell.

Washington's army was eventually saved by the heroic stand of Major Mordecai Gist's Maryland Regiment, which numbered no more than four hundred men but which held off some two thousand Scottish Highlanders and Hessians around the Vechte-Cortelyou House, a 1699 Dutch farmhouse (now known as the Old Stone House) that was reconstructed and stands today at Fifth Avenue and Third Street in Park Slope. Two hundred and fifty-six Marylanders were killed, more than one hundred were wounded or captured, and only nine, along with Major Gist, eventually rejoined the American forces. Washington is said to have watched the fight and lamented, "Good God! What brave fellows I must this day lose." His words are inscribed on architect Stanford White's memorial to the Marylanders, which stands at the base of Prospect Park's Lookout Hill as a testament to their valor. Their sacrifice was not in vain; it was crucial and may actu-ally have saved the Revolution. Washington's army was able to slip across the East River into Manhattan in a dense fog and lived to fight another day.

Nineteenth-century Brooklyn

By 1800 Brooklyn was an assortment of villages composed largely of the descendents of the original Dutch settlers. (African American slaves made up one-quarter of the population.) The villagers lived on fertile farms and pastures that stretched the length of Long Island. Farmers also drove their cattle across the shallow Buttermilk Channel from Brooklyn to Governors Island for its pristine pastureland.

The Brooklyn waterfront in the early nineteenth century was a cluster of taverns, stores, and houses around the ferry landing. The streets were unpaved, there were no streetlights or sidewalks, and pigs acted as garbage collectors (garbage collection did not start until 1824). The village had no market, no night watch, a police force "without organization…an apology for a fire department…and a government without the power or the will to properly enforce its ordi-nances. Those whose business called them abroad in the night, were obliged to carry their own lanterns, and cautiously to pick their wind-ing way through streets well nigh impassable from mud and mire."[4] Brooklyn didn't attract tourists; rather an 1818 guidebook of New York urged visitors "to flee the narrow, dirty and disagreeable place."[5]

The Maryland Monument, 1894.
Honoring heroes of the Revolution,
the monument stands proudly at
the foot of Lookout Hill.

But not all of Brooklyn was downtrodden. On the west side of Fulton Street—today's Brooklyn Heights—lived the "silk stocking gentry… men of order, and friends of good government."[6] There were pleasant country houses, like the one owned by Joseph Sprague at 115 Fulton Street, described in 1819 as being "surrounded by apple trees, open in front of the East River, and in the rear on vacant lots."[7] But Fulton Street was soon widened from a "little, narrow, crooked street—little more than a mere cow path" to a major thoroughfare, and by 1854 only one of these residences was still standing, the rest having given way to development.[8]

American inventor Robert Fulton's steam ferry began operations between Brooklyn and Manhattan in 1814, replacing vessels powered by horses on treadmills. It was a milestone in Brooklyn's expansion, turning this growing community into the nation's first suburb through frequent and fast ferry service across the East River. A young Olmsted was among those who in 1840 lived in Brooklyn and commuted to New York for work. The opening of the Erie Canal in 1825 had an even greater impact on growth, and almost overnight, commerce from the developing Midwest began flowing down the Hudson River to New York and Brooklyn. As trade expanded, New York replaced Boston and Philadelphia as the nation's leading port and commercial center. Raw materials, such as grain and flour, were imported from the west, and goods from overseas were shipped westward via the canal. New York quickly became the nation's largest city and was called "the London of the new world" by the London *Times*.[9]

The canal equally affected Brooklyn, which was incorporated as a city in 1834 and was expanding along the East River. Where cows once grazed, clattering factories spewed smoke, as the new city became a major port and manufacturing center. Its workers produced glass, cast iron, chemicals, glue, beer, and whiskey. Brooklyn's port was in fact larger and more modern than New York's, growing rapidly with shipyards and bustling with maritime traffic. Nowhere was the growth more evident than in the south side with the development of the Atlantic Dock area in the 1840s and the Erie Basin soon thereafter. It was at this time that the Red Hook area in south Brooklyn was transformed from a marshland into a busy industrial and residential area with new streets and lots awaiting development.

The Gowanus Canal was built in the late 1860s and extended a mile in length from Gowanus Bay to Douglass Street. To create this waterway, 1,700 acres in the south of Brooklyn were drained, opening up great areas of wetlands and marginal land to development and commerce. The canal, however, soon became the repository of all kinds of effluents from sewage to swamp water, which were thought to contribute to the marsh miasma that hung over sections of Brooklyn.

The consolidation of the cities of Brooklyn and Williamsburg in 1854 also assisted in Brooklyn's rapid growth. Throughout the nineteenth century, Brooklyn annexed more municipalities, including New Lots, Flatbush, Gravesend, New Utrecht, and Flatlands, until it consumed all of the land that now makes up Kings County.

Growth and Immigrants

The transformation of Brooklyn was not without challenges: immigrants poured into the city, and many of them lived in desperate poverty. Between 1820 and 1839, 667,000 immigrants came to the New York region. Between 1840 and 1859, 4,242,000 immigrants arrived in the United States, 75 percent of them entering through New York Harbor—as many as one-sixth stayed in the area, often residing in Brooklyn.

An English traveler, Isabella Bird, described these new Americans as they disembarked from "coffin ships"—referred to as such because so many died during the trans-Atlantic voyage:

> *The goods and chattels of the Irish appeared to consist principally of numerous red-haired, unruly children and ragged looking bundles tied around with rope. The Germans were generally ruddy and stout and took as much care of their substantial looking, well-corded, heavy chests as though they contained gold. The English appeared pale and debilitated, and sat helpless and weary-looking on their large blue boxes.*[10]

View of the Brooklyn waterfront from the Gowanus Heights, close to where Prospect Park would be constructed

Forty percent of the immigrants to New York were Irish fleeing the potato famine or the harsh British rule. Between 1845 and 1850 two million people left Ireland—one and a half million of whom came to the United States. Most were destitute, illiterate, and without skills, only qualified to take on low-paying jobs. During the same period, Germans migrated to the United States to escape the agricultural depression in their homeland and the retribution from the failed revolutions of 1848. Many were shopkeepers, intellectuals, and artisans who had supported progressive social programs. From England came unemployed factory workers and craftsmen as well as social reformers known as Chartists. In 1855 one-half of Brooklyn's residents were foreign born; of those, one-half were Irish, while German and English each constituted a little less than one-quarter.

The *New York Times* reported on the condition of impoverished people in Brooklyn: "In this city…are found a large class, mostly of foreign birth, who live in indolence, filth, and intemperence."[11] Many were homeless, many were vagabond children subject to diseases like cholera, diphtheria, smallpox, and typhoid. The common expectation that new immigrants would mingle easily with local inhabitants in one big melting pot was far from reality. The poor competed for jobs and housing, and violence was common. African Americans, because they were willing to work for lower wages than whites, were frequently attacked. Clashes also occurred regularly between native-born Americans and immigrants, between different immigrant groups, between Protestants and Catholics, and between members of different economic classes. The Atlantic Dock Company, in an effort to avoid a class war, announced that it would hire equal numbers of Irish and German workers, for example.

In 1840 Brooklyn covered twelve square miles and had a population of approximately thirty thousand. By 1869 the city was a bustling center of nearly four hundred thousand and had become the nation's third largest city, surpassed in number only by New York and Philadelphia. This phenomenal growth was not unique in the United States as urban areas expanded—Brooklyn's ascent just happened more quickly and took a terrible toll.

Urbanization, the Industrial Revolution, and increasing opposition to slavery gave rise to intellectual dissent about social conditions in the United States during the first half of the nineteenth century. Philosophers, writers, editors, and clergymen championed reformist causes. Henry David Thoreau, the author and philosopher, found faith in the simplicity of nature. Brooklyn's evangelical preacher Henry Ward Beecher, an avid abolitionist, staged mock auctions at his Plymouth Church to free runaway slaves. The philanthropist Charles Loring Brace, a friend and traveling companion of Olmsted's, founded the Children's Aid Society to provide shelter and food to orphaned and homeless children. William Cullen Bryant, poet and longtime editor of the *New York Evening Post*, opposed slavery and advocated for the right to strike and for collective bargaining. He, along with Andrew Jackson Downing, considered the father of American landscape design, ardently supported a great park for New York and, when combined with the efforts of others, would later make Central Park possible.

Vaux, and particularly Olmsted, fit easily into this group of reformers. Both men fervently believed that the young, American experiment of democracy could flourish in the great parks they would build.

The Need for Parks

During the 1820s the first attempt to create a Brooklyn public park, on a bluff in Brooklyn Heights overlooking the East River and Manhattan, failed because of a lack of consensus about size and location. In the absence of parks, American city dwellers flocked to large, recently established rural cemeteries for open space. In 1838 the two-hundred-acre rural Green-Wood Cemetery opened on the Gowanus Heights, an undeveloped section of the Harbor Hill Moraine not far from Mount Prospect and today's Prospect Park. Great cemeteries such as Green-Wood were built in several cities during this time to accommodate the affluent as smaller city church graveyards filled. Many rich-and-famous New York City and Brooklyn residents paid handsomely to spend eternity in Green-Wood, but the living also came in droves to experience the open grounds and some semblance of nature amid weeping statues and mausoleums. By 1860 Green-Wood Cemetery attracted five hundred thousand people a year, rivaling Niagara Falls as the country's most popular tourist site. For many New Yorkers, Green-Wood was the only place worth visiting in Brooklyn. As the popularity of cemeteries as places for country-like escapes grew, the pressure for cities to develop public parks intensified.

A few years before Green-Wood opened, New York Governor William L. Marcy appointed a commission to explore the possibility of a Brooklyn park system. In 1839 a plan for eleven new parks was

Green-Wood Cemetery's winding paths and sloping hillsides today

unveiled to the public but only a few were authorized—the approved list included Washington Park, now called Fort Greene Park. However, they were little more than postage stamps on the cityscape and hardly met the needs of Brooklyn's exploding population. Walt Whitman, editor of the *Brooklyn Daily Eagle* in the late 1840s and a vocal city-parks supporter, was particularly instrumental in the creation of Fort Greene Park. The site of Fort Putnam during the Revolution and the War of 1812, it was in danger of being leveled by developers. Whitman wrote, "First let it be settled that Fort Green [*sic*] shall be reserved for a public park."[12] It would be the "lungs" of the city with "pure air and play among the walks and grass…invigorating breezes…panoramic views."[13] It is believed that Whitman wrote *Leaves of Grass* (1855) in the newly opened park. Fort Greene Park was so actively used after it opened in 1850 that many argued for a larger park.

It was not until the late 1850s, however, with the development of Central Park, that Brooklynites acted zealously to build a park of similar proportions and stature, especially for the "common man." The wealthy could escape Brooklyn's sweltering summers by fleeing to resorts like Saratoga, and those in the Catskills and Adirondacks, but the working classes labored for long hours, six days a week, confined to the heat and squalor of the city. The New York State legislature authorized another Brooklyn Park Commission in 1859, which initially recommended that land be acquired for five new city parks. Of the five, two were to be large tracts: one measuring 1,300 acres near the Ridgewood Reservoir beyond Bushwick and the other, 267 acres, which would include the reservoir at Mount Prospect. Ridgewood Park was to be considerably larger, because the military wanted a sizeable parade ground for drills in the park, as was the custom of the time. The land proved to be too far from the center of Brooklyn, though, and in 1861 the tract around Mount Prospect was selected for a new park, which would be called Prospect Park. With this decision and the appointment of Brooklyn civic leader and park advocate James Stranahan as chairman of the Park Commission, Brooklyn was finally guaranteed its own sizable pleasure ground.

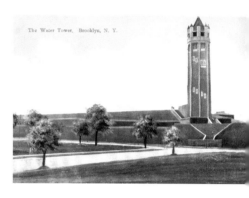

The reservoir and water tower at Mount Prospect were included in the original design for Prospect Park. In the 1930s the tower was demolished to make way for the Brooklyn Public Library.

The Role of the Commissions

While Olmsted, Vaux, and Stranahan can take credit for designing Prospect Park, New York State laws relating to the governance of municipalities and the long shadow of the Revolution greatly influenced, if not ensured, its existence. State-chartered local commissions, staffed by appointees rather than locally elected officials, controlled nearly every aspect of Brooklyn life in the first three-quarters of the nineteenth century. Also called "big boards," the first of these commissions was appointed in 1783 to compensate Brooklyn citizens whose property had been damaged during the Battle of Brooklyn and during the seven-year British occupation of New York and Long Island. British soldiers had ravaged the region, pillaging, appropriating livestock and crops, and clear-cutting the nearby forests for timber and firewood. By the mid-nineteenth century the New York State legislature was creating between twenty and fifty commissions annually that governed everything from city works and parks to the police and fire departments, leaving Brooklyn's mayor and the city's Common Council, the city's legislative body, with little authority. The *Eagle* likened the commissions to "tumors on a human being," adding that "the state legislature creates an infinite number of them, some of which escape the keenest scent of Albany correspondents, and are only known to be in existence when their operations in the city are discovered by the *Eagle* reporters."[14]

One commission was responsible for all health matters in Brooklyn, and its oversight included the condition and cleanliness of the city's streets. Another controlled many of the activities of the Common Council. The new Brooklyn Park Commission took over the operations of all city parks, including a small garden in front of city hall. Brooklyn's elected officials were not even permitted to control the maintenance of this tiny piece of greenery.

The commission and Stranahan were thus able to develop Prospect Park without political interference from local officials. With Stranahan in charge, Olmsted and Vaux did not need to worry about cost overruns and the financial hassles they had encountered with Central Park, where, according to Olmsted, Controller Andrew Haswell Green, who headed the project, would release "not a cent… from under his paw that is not wet with his blood and sweat."[15] They also would not have to deal with a complaining public as at Central Park. The Brooklyn Park Commission had absolute authority to issue bonds to pay for the park's construction, and city officials had no veto powers. The *Eagle* summed up the impact: "Perhaps no creation of the legislature rankled more in the hearts of Brooklyn officials than the Prospect Park commission. Its apparent immortality, magnificent independence, and the magnitude of the sums which it expended all contributed to its unpopularity."[16]

Egbert Viele's Plan

In 1860 the Park Commission hired Central Park's original engineer-in-chief, Egbert Ludovicus Viele, whose design for Central Park was later displaced by the one created by Olmsted and Vaux, to craft a plan for Prospect Park. His design was for a much smaller park than what exists today.

A graduate of the United States Military Academy at West Point, Viele held many posts during his life: he was a regular army officer, the chief engineer for New Jersey, a Union brigadier general during the Civil War, a topographer for New York City, the city park commissioner, and a one-term member of Congress. He was more engineer than landscape designer in his sensibilities: his scheme for Prospect Park did not include a lake, a beautifully sculpted ravine, or waterfalls. The Lullwater, Music Island, the Oriental Pavilion, and the rustic shelters would not have existed in Viele's Prospect Park.

Viele's plan consisted of 320 acres stretching from today's Ninth Street and Prospect Park West in Park Slope east beyond Flatbush Avenue to encompass what was then known as the East Side Lands. (The two-hundred-foot Mount Prospect was a part of the East Side

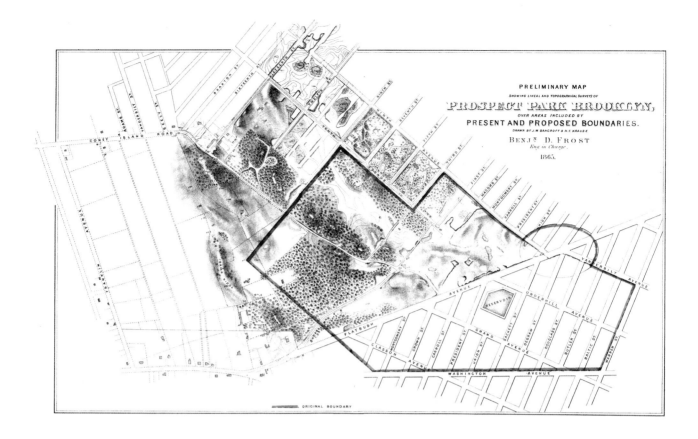

PRELIMINARY MAP

SHOWING LINEAL AND TOPOGRAPHICAL SURVEYS OF

PROSPECT PARK BROOKLYN,

OVER AREAS INCLUDED BY

PRESENT AND PROPOSED BOUNDARIES.

DRAWN BY J. M. BANCROFT & H. F. KRAUSE

BENJ.ⁿ D. FROST
Eng in Charge.

1865.

ORIGINAL BOUNDARY

Lands and offered panoramic views.) Today the Brooklyn Museum, the Brooklyn Botanic Garden, the Brooklyn Central Library, and Mount Prospect Park occupy most of the East Side Lands. The summit of Mount Prospect was the site of one of the city's two receiving reservoirs, built for the new water system. One rationale for extending the park to Mount Prospect was to protect the water supply from the contamination that would be expected if the area was developed for residential use.

Viele extolled the natural beauty of the park site: "The succession of beautifully-wooded hills and broad green meadows, interrupted here and there by a natural pond of water….These offer features of attraction which require but little aid from art to fit it for all the purposes of health and recreation, to which it is to be devoted."[17] This was a swipe at Olmsted and Vaux's 1858 Central Park design, which enhanced what nature already provided with the creation of a lake, hills, and lawns from previously fallow ground. The cost for similarly embellishing Prospect Park would be significant, Viele warned, and it would be "an infringement upon good taste, and upon that regard for the beauties of nature possessed by every cultivated mind." He noted that "artificial constructions would defeat the primary object of the park as a rural resort, where the people of all classes, escaping from the glare, and glitter, and the turmoil of the city, might find relief for the mind."[18] Viele also criticized the buildings and structures in Central Park, which he thought were artificial and conformed to designs that would soon be out of fashion.

Egbert Viele's park plan is outlined in red on this map of the area.

No love was lost between Viele and Olmsted and Vaux. Viele accused the two of copying many elements of his rejected plan in their design of Central Park, and he reacted the same way to their Prospect Park scheme. There were indeed similarities between Viele's 1860 and later Olmsted and Vaux plans for Prospect Park. Viele's design set the main entrance in the vicinity of Vanderbilt and Flatbush Avenues near the present Grand Army Plaza. His proposal also contained a meadow, a pond, and carriage drives, and included walks, a forest, and a flower garden with curving paths next to the reservoir.

The most significant differences between the two plans were the size of the park and the treatment of Flatbush Avenue. In Viele's plan, the avenue was incorporated as a one-hundred-foot-wide, raised thoroughfare running diagonally through the center of the park. The engineer admitted that Flatbush Avenue "might be regarded as a serious blemish to the beauty of the finished park," but he noted that it would obviate the need for cross streets that cut through the park to connect the city to the suburbs as development eventually spread out.[19] He also argued that Flatbush Avenue offered magnificent views of Brooklyn, the harbor in one direction and the ocean in the other.

The Land before the Park

Viele's characterization of the Prospect Park site as having wooded hills and broad green meadows was true to an extent, but it did not adequately describe the land. One Brooklyn resident called Mount Prospect "beautiful" but considered the surrounding area altogether unhealthy and undesirable. In a letter to the *Eagle* he wrote, "Those heights…must be cut down, the range of hills…must be more or less leveled, the bowls or depressed spots filled up, must be well-drained and sewered, streets must be opened and paved before the curse of the place, miasma, the producer of fever and ague, diarrhea, dysentery, etc., will be exterminated.…It is an unhealthy region, a plague spot, as those who have tried to live there have found to their sorrow."[20] The *Eagle* called the ground "sterile land occupied only by goats and squatters."[21]

Stranahan knew it would be difficult to reshape the northern part of the park site: "The ground we had to operate upon was in part a quagmire, and elsewhere consisted largely of a tough, endured clay, packed with stone, and requiring to be moved by the crow and pick. The whole district of our earlier operations was indeed a desert of the most disagreeable character, rugged, treeless, mutilated and laying bare to the avenues."[22] Furthermore, animals, mostly cows and pigs, from nearby farms roamed freely and constantly had to be rounded up and returned to their owners. Goats rambled through the woods and over the meadows, eating foliage from trees and shrubs. As late as 1872, farm animals were being impounded. The take that year included forty-four pigs, thirty-five goats, eighteen cows, and twenty-three horses.

Local residents used the area for other purposes as well. The ground behind Litchfield Villa, now part of the Long Meadow, was an athletic field pounded bald by many football and baseball games.

A patch of countryside would be transformed into a great city park.

Hicks Post ran his "little snuggery," the Valley Grove Tavern, near Battle Pass. It was a favorite stop for day-trippers on their way to Coney Island. Another watering hole a few hundred yards to the northwest was run by Mr. McCarty, who took his nickname, "Major," not from a previous military rank but from his "voluminous nasal protuberance," according to an 1891 *Eagle* article.[23]

Portions of the grounds of the new park had already been slated for residential development. The south end of the Long Meadow was being prepared for building sites and future streets. Other sections, mostly around the Lake, consisted of farms owned by established Brooklyn families, such as the Willinks, the Martensens, and the Murphys. In 1860 much of the area that is today's Park Slope and Flatbush was open farmland. There were few buildings, and most were from the Colonial period. Some of the area closest to the park was densely wooded; the rest was maintained in orchards and wheat fields. The land near today's Gowanus Canal was dotted with salt marshes and meadows. The *Eagle* recalled that bygone era: "Throughout the slope [Park Slope] everything savored of 'ye olden tyme,' and while the farmer held the plough, cattle roamed about the slope, and several old-fashioned saw and grist mills, run by ponds still partially visible, converted trees into building material and grain into flour, to the profit of the miller and the convenience of the industrious husbandman."[24]

In 1861, before Viele's plan could proceed beyond the initial planning, the Civil War broke out and delayed construction of the park for five years. It also doomed Viele's design. His arrogant demeanor did not help his cause—he was a stern military type who insisted upon being addressed as Colonel—nor did his plan for a military parade ground where the Park Commission had wanted a meadow. But even without the construction moratorium imposed by the war, the development of the park would have been delayed until 1864, when the commission finally took possession of the farmland leading toward Flatbush village. That same year the military selected the land adjacent to Prospect Park for use as a parade ground, and plans for the 1,300-acre park at Ridgewood were abandoned.

The war gave the Park Commission four years to study alternate designs, while the ongoing development of Central Park pressured them into action. "Indeed, we in Brooklyn were already feeling the consequences of its Central Park construction in a manner not at all satisfactory to us," Stranahan noted.[25] Mostly, there was a growing sense that Prospect Park should be larger than originally envisioned. After the war Stranahan called for a new design competition, and in 1865 the commission embraced the plan offered by Calvert Vaux.

STRANAHAN, VAUX, AND OLMSTED

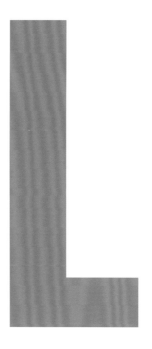

UCK, PROVIDENCE, OR MAYBE AN ALIGNMENT
of the stars brought James S. T. Stranahan, Calvert Vaux, and Frederick Law Olmsted together to conceive, design, and build Prospect Park between 1860 and 1872. It was a rare association. Alter the circumstances of their lives even slightly, and Prospect Park as we know it today would not exist. Stranahan might not have chaired the Park Commission in 1860—he wasn't even a member in early 1859. Had the Civil War not been fought, Brooklyn undoubtedly would have a less splendid public space designed by Egbert Viele. If Vaux hadn't insisted that a reluctant Olmsted return from California to help build the park, it would probably be an inferior landmark.

Stranahan, Vaux, and Olmsted each brought different talents to the task of shaping and building Prospect Park. Stranahan, an astute businessman, had the power, vision, and determination to push the project against much opposition. Vaux had the architectural training and experience as well as the aesthetic temperament and skills of an accomplished artist to create a splendid design. Olmsted was expert at managing large numbers of men, and his farming background provided a solid understanding of horticulture and a sense of landscape. More importantly, Olmsted had the foresight to see Prospect Park, and all parks, as an antidote to the stresses of the new industrial world. He and Vaux were among a growing intellectual elite who understood that the Industrial Revolution was reshaping rural American life through the rise of burgeoning urban centers. Change was occurring at a rapid pace, and these three men were at the forefront of a movement to dampen its excesses.

James Stranahan

Time has obscured Stranahan's colossal presence and influence in nineteenth-century Brooklyn, but for fifty years—up until his death in 1898—he was a major player in its growth from a small trading village to a vibrant metropolis with more than a million people. Moreover, his own life mirrored the transformations taking place in the United States: born in 1808, he began as a farm boy, became an adventurer of the unexplored western frontier, then worked as a factory manager as industrialization altered the United States, and finally thrived as an entrepreneur and a public servant in his beloved Brooklyn. More than anyone else, he is responsible for Prospect Park.

Stranahan came to Brooklyn in 1844 as a young man, seeking to expand his fortune and opportunities after pursuing business ventures in railroads. The city's rapid growth benefited fleet-footed businessmen, and he soon had a hand in many facets of local commerce, from bank boards to insurance companies. He became a principal owner of the Atlantic Dock Company and owned the Union Ferry Company. He was also instrumental in saving the Brooklyn Navy Yard when the government proposed moving it to New London, Connecticut.

PREVIOUS
Concert Grove, 1890s

Undeterred by how the Brooklyn Bridge would affect his ferry company, he became a prime advocate for the bridge's construction. Stranahan's name appears, third down from the top, on the plaque commemorating the bridge's opening in 1883, during which he was master of ceremonies. He also believed that more than a bridge was necessary to link New York and Brooklyn; for many years he advocated consolidation of the two cities, which was achieved nine months before he died.

The fact that Brooklyn was considered a cultural wasteland by New Yorkers, who even regarded its citizens as lesser beings, inspired Stranahan to enrich his city through the advancement of the arts. He was instrumental in building libraries and schools and was a founder of the Brooklyn Collegiate and Polytechnic Institute along with the Brooklyn Academy of Music. But it was his vision of a public space to rival Central Park that was his most fervent endeavor. A magnificent Brooklyn park, he advocated, would attract prosperous Manhattan residents, increase tax revenues, and foster real estate and economic development. It would also be a civilizing force as it became part of the city's fabric. "The health, strength, comfort, morality and future wealth of the city would be promoted by building a suitable park," he said.[1] He was concerned that Brooklyn would become "a second rate suburb of the greater city" without a counterpart to Central Park.

Prospect Park soon became Stranahan's greatest passion and personal triumph. Although Olmsted and Vaux are the park's marquis figures, it was really Stranahan's shrewd political maneuvering and iron will that made the park a reality. Olmsted and Vaux left soon after Prospect Park officially opened in 1872, but Stranahan stayed on to lead the commission for another ten years and ensure that the original design remained unchanged. The businessman showed mettle in his dealings with Prospect Park detractors. Skeptics soon realized that Stranahan wasn't just one member of the Park Commission—he *was* the commission, and his rule was unquestioned. Mayors and aldermen could object to the park's soaring costs and to Stranahan's perceived autocratic leadership, but they could not challenge the state commission's ultimate authority.

From the outset there were complaints, often furious ones. The *Brooklyn Daily Eagle* stated that an expenditure Stranahan called a "mere trifle" could range from $200 to $200,000.[2] While the 1860 act authorizing a park established that the total cost could not exceed $300,000, the final bill soared to $9,919,370, an astronomical sum in the 1870s.[3] Mayor John W. Hunter (who was in office from 1874 to 1875) was particularly vexed by Stranahan's ways and ranted constantly as he tried to reduce costs. Hunter's complaints became so persistent that the *Eagle* mocked him publicly:

> *For months and years this hated reign*
> *Has been a nightmare on his Hunter's brain*
> *And like the sleeper that's distressed*
> *And is with horrid dreams oppressed,*
> *Cries Stranahan!*

HON. J. S. T. STRANAHAN.

Brooklyn's biggest booster, James Stranahan was the driving force behind many cultural institutions.

When through the Park he Hunter madly flies
With muttered curse and flashing eyes,
He sees not those who there may ride,
But pointing to the Eastern Side,
Cries Stranahan![4]

Despite his frustration, the mayor was fascinated by Stranahan and admired his ability to sway those around him:

I would like to be one of the Park Commission for a few weeks just
to see if Stranahan could mesmerize me as he seems to every man
that is brought into public relations with him.…How on earth can
a single man be stronger than parties, stronger than laws, stronger than
the almost universal will of the whole city; how can he be silently, gently,
yet undisputedly despotic, alike in successive Legislatures where he
has no seat, and among associate Commissioners of equal position…;
how in short, can he have his own way all the time, in spite of all
possible odds against him?[5]

So how, in fact, did a man who started life as a rube, snorted snuff, and, in old age, still lit his cigars by striking a match on the sole of his boot, accomplish so many gargantuan tasks? The *Eagle* offered an answer: "Mr. Stranahan is essentially a man of grand ideas; his confidence in the future is boundless; nothing appears impossible to him; the project in hand appears to him the only project worthy of consideration."[6] A short account of his life may help explain his success with Prospect Park.

Born in Peterboro in upstate New York and raised among "plain country folk," Stranahan liked to say he was born in the same year as the "three greatest rascals who ever lived: Louis Napoleon, Jefferson Davis and Andrew Johnson."[7] His father was a farmer and miller, and farming had been in his Scotch-Irish blood since the seventeenth century when his ancestors came to America. The elder Stranahan died when his son was eight, and Stranahan quickly assumed responsibilities well beyond his age. When his mother remarried, he helped maintain his stepfather's farm, sometimes herding sheep and cattle to markets in New York City and Boston.[8]

Stranahan had an adventurous spirit and, like Olmsted, experimented with a number of professions before finding his calling. He taught school for a year during an era when teachers were often the same age as their oldest students, before pursuing a short career in civil engineering. He tried his hand in the fur trade and, in 1829, trekked through uncharted wilderness from western New York State to the upper Great Lakes in order to establish links with the region's Native American tribes.[9] Anyone who tramped through that area during the early nineteenth century was exceedingly resourceful and courageous. Many of the tribes living there had sided with the British during the American Revolution and the War of 1812, and war erupted between American settlers and some of the tribes in the same countryside in 1832.

Soon thereafter, Stranahan was city manager for the factory town of Florence, New York, at the behest of Gerrit Smith, an eminent capitalist, social reformer, and philanthropist. He was so successful at this position that he was elected to the state legislature in 1838. Relinquishing politics two years later, he traveled to Newark, New Jersey, and laid the foundations of his fortune by constructing railroads. Opting for stock certificates in lieu of wages, he eventually owned large portions of several railroads. He would follow this formula in later business ventures, adding to his sizable wealth.

From Newark Stranahan relocated to Brooklyn, then a city of about thirty thousand. "It was all country," he remembered in 1891.[10] The city charter was only ten years old, and there was no town hall. The financial Panic of 1837 had curtailed plans for a stately government seat, and all that graced the triangular plot where the current Borough Hall now stands was a one-story wall. The entirety of Brooklyn consisted of an area between Court Street and the East River. "There were no street cars. Everybody lived within walking distance of the two ferries or else rode up and down Fulton Street in a line of omnibuses (horse drawn) which were the only public conveyances."[11] Brooklyn was caught in the orbit of New York City, which pulsed with energy just across the East River, and Stranahan perceived that with the right touch, that city's energy and wealth could flow into his new hometown.

The businessman found opportunity everywhere and became associated with the Atlantic Dock Company, which developed a forty-acre port along Brooklyn's waterfront. He took a controlling interest in the company and created the world's most technologically advanced ship-loading system, a huge grain elevator that was so efficient that the *Eagle* could barely contain its amazement. "The elevator lifts corn quicker than Jersey whiskey can raise an inferno," a reporter noted.[12] A shipment of grain from Brooklyn could be loaded and delivered to Germany faster across three thousand miles of ocean than a similar shipment could be sent from England, where grain ships were loaded using shovels.

In 1848 Stranahan was elected to the Brooklyn Board of Aldermen; in 1850 he ran for mayor and lost; and in 1854 he ran for Congress as a Whig and won. Congressman Stranahan served only one term, but in 1858 he was back in the public eye, heading the commission reorganizing the metropolitan police force, and in 1860 and 1864 he was a delegate at the Republican National Convention, where he supported Abraham Lincoln. It was around this time, in 1859, that he was appointed to the Brooklyn Park Commission, becoming its chairman in 1860.

Both abolitionists, Stranahan and his first wife, Marianne Fitch, were also prominent figures in Civil War relief programs, working with the Brooklyn Sanitary Fair to raise more than $400,000 for the United States Sanitary Commission. Marianne died in 1866, and Stranahan, who supported women's rights, encouraged his second wife, Clara C. Harrison, to found Barnard College, New York's first women's college. In Clara, Stranahan had a partner of high intellect

and drive whose cultured background may have played a part in smoothing over any of the rough-hewn traits of his rural upbringing.

During his ninety years, Stranahan earned numerous monikers. Though some were unflattering, those that were favorable indicated his high position in the community. Besides being called the "first citizen of Brooklyn," he was dubbed "the magician" and "the wizard" by the *Eagle*, which peppered the paper's columns with descriptions of his legendary ability to shepherd various projects to fruition through the maze of political intrigues, personal enemies, and bureaucratic roadblocks.[13]

Prospect Park was Stranahan's pride. "He watched the park with the solicitude of a mother watching a sleeping baby," said the Reverend R. S. Storrs, a Brooklyn pastor and Stranahan's friend. "There was hardly a tree removed or a tree planted, hardly a drive or walk laid out, or a bit of shrubbery planted here and there that his personal attention was not given. It is very well to say that they had the best landscape architects in the world but they could not have done anything without him."[14] Every day that Stranahan was in Brooklyn, he attempted to take a carriage ride through the park.

After 1871, with the park nearing completion, complaints about the costs diminished. The people of Brooklyn loved their new park, and the *Eagle* gave Stranahan full credit for its creation: "Prospect Park, as it exists to-day, would never have had an existence except for Mr. Stranahan."[15] At a Hamilton Club dinner held in his honor in 1883, the members decided that a statue of Stranahan, later sculpted by Frederick MacMonnies, would be placed in the park. Four mayors, MacMonnies, his mentor—Augustus Saint-Gaudens—and a crowd of well-wishers were on hand at the unveiling in 1891. In bronze, the statue of Stranahan shows him striding along in street attire: a waistcoat and double-breasted frock coat. He holds a silk top hat in his right hand; in his left hand, tightly fitted with a glove, he clutches a walking stick, and he has an overcoat draped over his arm. He is depicted as an elderly man, still handsome, with a slight paunch, balding on top but with thick locks flowing halfway down the nape of his neck. His forehead is broad, his chin prominent, his nose Romanesque, and his countenance firm and calm. Stranahan quipped that unveiling a likeness of a living person was a risky thing, knowing the frailty of human nature.[16]

Stranahan continued working into his late eighties and went to his cubbyhole office at the Atlantic Dock everyday. Around the time he signed the company over to the McIntyre Syndicate, his health began to decline and he died three years later. He was a giant among men, and the *Eagle* devoted several pages to his obituary. On the day of his death, September 3, 1898, the *New York Times* remembered him fondly: "He linked his own personal fortunes with the fortunes of the City of Churches Brooklyn and the measure of success that attended his plans was but an infinitesimal part of the advantage that accrued to the city through his business sagacity and public spirit."[17]

The entire city stopped to mourn. Dr. H. P. Dewey, pastor of the Church of the Pilgrims, which Stranahan had attended, spoke of his deeds:

Mr. Stranahan had the genius of accomplishment—of accomplishment on a vast scale. With vaulting imagination he conceived large things; and with sanity of judgment, loftiness of purpose, assertiveness and steadfastness of will, and the rare gift of leadership, he could waken into realization what the dream had seen....Through him as originator or as efficient supporter, two miles of docks were laid upon our shores, a bridge was thrown across yonder river, educational institutions were established, and the people were given an inexhaustible and perpetual source of instruction and enjoyment and health in a park of surpassing beauty, which, as a voice familiar to this congregation has described it, lies as "an emerald on the city's brow." [18]

Stranahan took a last ride through Prospect Park in his own funeral cortege, which entered at the Plaza, passed along West Drive, and exited at a southern entrance on its way to Green-Wood Cemetery, where he is interred. Park employees and old friends lined the way to pay their last respects. Prospect Park was Stranahan's magnum opus, and his epitaph— the same as Christopher Wren's at St. Paul's Cathedral in London —is engraved on the base of his statue at the park's entrance just off Grand Army Plaza: *"Lector si monumentum requires circumspice."* (Reader, if you want my monument, look around you.)

Calvert Vaux

Stranahan had used his political and personal influence to build a great public park for Brooklyn, but Vaux was the man whose plan shaped the raw acres of land—hills, forest, farmland, and bogs—into Prospect Park. Vaux is the lesser-known member of the Olmsted/ Vaux partnership, yet he was an equal collaborator—some say the principal designer of Prospect Park. Vaux greatly improved Viele's original plan and suggested the addition of several hundred contiguous acres toward Flatbush for a lake. The boundaries and dimensions of Prospect Park today remain essentially the same as Vaux laid out in a rough sketch for Stranahan in 1865.

Vaux was not only a formally trained architect with experience in landscape design, but also an accomplished artist with an eye for the subtleties of nature that he committed to canvas and later transposed onto his landscapes. He studied and practiced architecture in his native England before emigrating to the United States in 1850 as an associate of Andrew Jackson Downing. Downing met Vaux in 1850 at a London art exhibit that included the latter's paintings, and he saw that Vaux's artistic sensibilities would fit well with his own work. As he wanted to expand his landscape design practice and needed a trained architect, he hired Vaux on the spot to join his firm in Newburgh, New York.

During this era, landscapes were depicted largely as idealized and romanticized visions: mystical forests, sparkling lakes, and pristine meadows brushed and dabbed in rich hues or in subtle pastels. These works of art—many from the painters of the Hudson River School art movement—were often the only still-life representations of nature

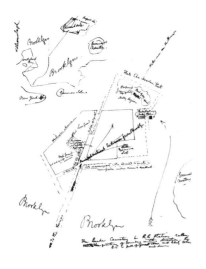

Calvert Vaux's 1865 sketch of his recommended boundaries for Prospect Park

available to landscape designers to reference. Vaux's own paintings played an important role in his career. Through his paintings and sketches, Vaux demonstrated a close kinship with the natural world. "Mr. Vaux was profoundly in love with nature and endeavored to study and comprehend her in all her moods," wrote Samuel Parsons, a colleague in Vaux's architectural firm, adding that Vaux could "divine the secret of a particular bit of Nature's design and use the idea in his own composition so that one would feel the scene to be thoroughly natural, familiar even, and yet transfigured and elevated by higher emotions."[19] Vaux loved to amble through the stunning and craggy beauty of the Adirondacks, stopping to sketch and paint "the rugged mountain slope or moss-covered rock, the dark pool reflecting overhanging trees, or the intricate interlacing of the foliage of some old monarch of the forest."[20] His renderings for the Central Park proposal helped sway the New York Park Commission to favor Vaux and Olmsted during the design competition.

Vaux had the ability to design Prospect Park, but he lacked Olmsted's hard-nosed management skills to implement his plan and urged his former partner to return to Brooklyn to assist in the construction: "I felt my incapability of going it alone," he told Olmsted.[21] Vaux hoped Olmsted would supervise the construction while he concentrated on design. It is Vaux who is responsible for the handsome arches, the Dairy, the Oriental Pavilion, the Concert Grove House, the rustic wooden shelters, and the bridges that blend so seamlessly into the park landscape. But in enlisting the assertive and driven Olmsted, he acquiesced to second billing, and throughout the remainder of his life he lived, largely by his own design, in Olmsted's shadow.

Vaux, born in 1824, was a diminutive man at four feet eleven inches. He had a ruddy face framed by a well-coiffed beard and a shock of thick, dark, wavy hair covering a receding hairline, as he peered out at the world through the pince-nez balanced on the bridge of his nose. He entered the world into a comfortable life in London, although the family's circumstances were diminished when his father, an apothecary and surgeon, died of a stroke when Vaux was just eight.

Nevertheless, he was still able to attend the exclusive Merchant Taylors' School, where he excelled in Latin, Greek, geography, writing, and mathematics. In 1843 he left school to study under architect Lewis Nockalls Cottingham, who worked in the English Gothic Revival style and was known for having restored the Magdalen College chapel at the University of Oxford as well as the Rochester Cathedral. Vaux emulated Cottingham's style well into his career in the many country mansions he designed to blend into the Hudson River Valley landscape.

During his apprenticeship Vaux befriended fellow architect and colleague George Truefitt, who encouraged his drawing talents. The high point of their friendship was a walking tour of several European countries in 1846, during which the two sketched and observed the relationships of buildings to the land. About this, Vaux later wrote:

In Italy or the East the air…allows remote objects to be very clearly seen.…But it is, at the same time, so suffused with an attenuated, almost imperceptible, hazy medium, that the direct glaring rays of the sun are subdued and softened before they meet the eye, and a delicate gradation of perspective distance, with an agreeable variety of harmonious half-tints, is the natural result. In America this seldom occurs. The supply of light is usually free from any mellowing veil: it is, therefore, colorless or white, and very decided in its pictorial character.[22]

Vaux brought his skills as an architect and artist to his partnership with Frederick Law Olmsted.

Vaux later adapted his architectural and landscape designs in the United States to "rather relieve than increase this fatiguing effect."[23] During his apprenticeship he was also a friend of the well-known English architect George Godwin, who preached that landscape design was a talent learned, not one that was given.

The life of a professional architect in mid-nineteenth-century Britain was uncertain, and Vaux supplemented his income doing odd jobs, including a stint as a calligrapher, lettering signs and maps. His special talent was writing backwards, which saved time during the printing process. Under these circumstances, Vaux gladly accepted Downing's offer of employment after their first meeting in 1850. Vaux's first exposure to Downing's work was when he arrived at Highland Gardens in Newburgh, New York, the landscape designer's "villa," which was described as a "miniature paradise."[24] An orchard bounded the west side of the five acres and a vineyard, the eastern side. Ornamental grounds enclosed the house, which was surrounded by shadowy pathways, fragrant beds of moss and thyme, and log and bark shelters. The scene resembled the Prospect Park Ravine with a path winding through dense foliage, past a rustic bench fashioned from tree branches and a small shelter with a conical roof.

Generally known by the public as the advocate of what was considered good taste, Downing was concerned with more than just designing beautiful grounds. He believed that the working classes should be exposed to the elegant standards espoused by the wealthy, and that the rich were not the only group that could appreciate beauty. His magazine, *Horticulturist—A Journal of Rural Art and Rural Taste*, published between 1846 and 1852, promoted this ideal and offered readers information on a range of subjects, such as how to plant gladiolus bulbs, graft pear trees, and select the appropriate garden furniture. It was through the magazine that Vaux first met Olmsted, who had written articles for it.

Vaux quickly climbed the ranks at Downing's firm and became a partner, designing country estates where the landscape was critical. One of these early undertakings was Mathew Vassar's Poughkeepsie manor (1852), described as the "realization of a painter's dream and the embodiment of a poet's glowing thought."[25] The design incorporated an abundance of undulating lines, trees grouped and scattered throughout, and drives and other design features adapted to suit the terrain. Ironically, today many would call these elements "Olmstedian." Vaux and Downing also worked on improving the public grounds surrounding the Smithsonian Institution and the White House.

Downing advocated for a large park in New York City, and when, in 1851, he learned that a 160-acre parcel was being considered for that purpose, he called for the acquisition of a much larger plot of at least 500 acres. Had Downing lived, he and Vaux—not Olmsted and Vaux—would likely have designed Central Park, and possibly Prospect Park. And Vaux's reputation might have eclipsed Olmsted's. Downing was killed in an 1852 Hudson River steamboat accident, however—thousands mourned his passing at age thirty-seven.

Downing had a lasting influence on both Olmsted and Vaux. Olmsted dedicated the second volume of his book, *Walks and Talks of an American Farmer in England* (1852), to Downing, and Vaux named one of his sons after him.[26] Olmsted and Vaux together carried Downing's vision of public parks to new heights in their own works, incorporating many of his design ideas and concepts, especially the belief that parks had a democratizing and civilizing impact on urban life.

Vaux's career and life continued to flourish after Downing's death. In 1854 he married Mary Swan McEntee, the younger sister of Jervis McEntee, a Hudson River School landscape painter. The couple settled in Newburgh and started a family: first two sons, followed by two daughters. Vaux also finished his book, *Villas and Cottages* (1857), which includes a selection of the houses and grounds he and Downing designed for families of varying incomes.

When Vaux moved his offices to New York City, he and Mary bought a house on the New Jersey Palisades overlooking the Hudson River, just north of New York City and opposite Yonkers. A visitor recalled climbing to the house along a winding road to the top of the cliffs to an area filled with wildflowers, pastures, swamp, and forest. Just beyond Vaux's house, where every window and door opened to woods, were views of the Hudson and hills rolling into the distance. Long Island and the Sound were visible on clear days. The house was decorated with "delicate vases, rich hangings, quaint woodwork, landscape paintings and books." Vaux also built a small summer cottage nearby on the edge of the Palisades that he called Restawhile. It was evocative of the same tranquility and intellectual atmosphere of the Vaux household. He additionally kept a small pied-à-terre on Tenth Street in New York City, which he used to host influential businessmen, professionals, social reformers, and artistic types, as he had a particular affinity for painters, poets, and writers. The architect H. Van Buren Magonigle, a colleague, recalled that Vaux had the soul and demeanor of Lord Byron, and that he belonged to "a school of romanticists even then fast vanishing."[27]

Vaux associated with many well-known contemporary painters, including McEntee and fellow Hudson River School artist Frederic Edwin Church, whose rich landscapes may have stirred the imagination of Olmsted and Vaux when they designed Prospect Park's meandering Long Meadow and Ravine. He also associated with the poet and critic Charles Clarence Stedman; Edwin Lawrence Godkin, editor of the *Nation*; Parke Godwin, editor of the *Evening Post*; and George William Curtis, editor of *Harper's New Monthly Magazine*.

Like Olmsted, as a member of the prestigious Century Association in New York, a group dedicated to the furthering of literature and the fine arts, he was undoubtedly familiar with artist Winslow Homer and writers Henry Adams and William Dean Howells, who were also members.

Vaux lamented that his adopted country lacked culture and an appreciation for the arts. The United States, he noted in *Villas and Cottages*, is "a dollar-making country, with restricted opportunities for popular, artistic education." In fact, he claimed that "architects are not at present, in the majority of cases, born or bred in the United States."[28] To counter this deficiency and to promote public awareness of architects and architecture, Vaux became one of the founding members of the American Institute of Architects (AIA) in 1857. At this time, masons, bricklayers, and carpenters were all folded under the general title of architect, and the AIA sought to elevate both the standards and the standing of the profession.

As an architect, Vaux changed age-old domestic concepts: he proposed libraries with inlaid bookcases, dining rooms for festive dinners on the main floor (rather than in the dark basement as was the custom), and parlors—the most elegant room of the house— for use as the family's living room and not just for formal entertainment. He set the standard for the Victorian Gothic style with his verandas, steep gables, deeply hooded and bay windows, and porte cocheres (porticos for discharging carriage passengers). Vaux favored using rough stone, brick, and slate in his designs and was concerned with the color of materials, even that of the mortar, and how it changed as a result of weathering. But the main tenet of his designs was that the landscape was paramount and that buildings must blend into their surroundings. "Woods, fields, mountains and rivers will be more important than the houses built on them," he noted.[29]

In 1856 he and an associate, Jacob Wrey Mould, designed the opulent home of John A. C. Gray, a retired dry-goods magnate and a Central Park commissioner, whom Vaux had befriended. In 1860 Gray introduced Vaux to Stranahan, who was studying various sites for a new Brooklyn park at the time, and only five years later Stranahan would invite him to create a plan for Prospect Park.

In the 1870s Vaux designed the original buildings of the Metropolitan Museum of Art and the American Museum of Natural History. The strength of his Metropolitan Museum design, completed with Mould, is visible in the museum's Lehman Court, where the former west facade with its Gothic arches has been exposed. A similar arch—of rusticated, contrasting granite—formed part of the top story of the museum's exterior and was recently uncovered just off of the grand staircase leading to the second-floor galleries. With its pointed shape and rich use of color and texture, the arch represents the High Victorian style of architecture—a style that declined in popularity and was considered old-fashioned by the time the building was erected. A *New York Times* critic ravaged Vaux's work: "The museum is a forcible example of architectural ugliness fit only for a winter garden or a railway depot."[30]

The Metropolitan Museum of Art's first building in Central Park, c. 1880, designed by Vaux and Jacob Wrey Mould. © The Metropolitan Museum of Art.

In the years following the opening of Prospect Park Vaux continued to design estates and their grounds, including a sumptuous mansion for Samuel J. Tilden, a corporate lawyer, former New York governor, and erstwhile presidential candidate. But by the 1880s, his landscape career was in decline and he took the position of chief architect for the New York City Park Commission and designed a few smaller city parks.[31]

The partnership between Olmsted and Vaux, forged by their collaboration on Central and Prospect Parks and numerous other projects, endured for sixteen years, from 1857 to 1873. Their final project—in collaboration with their sons John Charles Olmsted and Downing Vaux—was the 1889 design of the thirty-five-acre Andrew Jackson Downing Park in Newburgh.

In 1895 Vaux's body was found near a pier in Gravesend Bay. The cause of death was never determined, but there are suggestions that the seventy-one-year-old Vaux took his own life because of his declining health and reputation. It would be one hundred years before the city of New York honored his work in naming the Calvert Vaux Park, overlooking Gravesend Bay.

Frederick Law Olmsted

The man whom today many refer to simply as FLO had no formal training in landscape architecture and once remarked that he "had no more idea of ever being a park-maker than of taking command of the channel fleet."[32] Olmsted held a succession of jobs before finding a passion for landscape design, and even then it was a decade in developing. While Vaux was working with well-respected architects and perfecting his vocation, Olmsted was variously an apprentice surveyor, store clerk, merchant seaman, gentleman farmer, journalist, and author before becoming superintendent and codesigner of Central Park in the late 1850s and early 1860s. In 1861 he left the park to work as general secretary of the United States Sanitary Commission (a forerunner of the American Red Cross), and in 1863 he became manager of a California mining operation.

In 1866, at age forty-three, he returned to New York City from the West Coast and began to work with Vaux on the construction of Prospect Park, launching the career that would make him famous. The years Olmsted spent building Central and Prospect Parks were, he said, his graduate-school education in landscape design. But it was a career that almost did not happen.

Vaux had urged Olmsted to return to Brooklyn from his job directing the failing Mariposa Mining Estate in California—not far from the magnificent Yosemite Valley—to help build Prospect Park. Olmsted had freelanced on several landscape projects while in California, including the design for a college and a cemetery, and he had been the chairman of the commission overseeing the new Yosemite State Park. He declined Vaux's initial offer, but Vaux persisted and played on Olmsted's vanity and passion for social reform, insisting that he could transform his democratic ideals into trees and dirt and practice what he called "sylvan art" while developing a park open to all ranks of society.[33] He stated that the fate of the parks movement was vital to the progress of the Republic and convinced Olmsted that his true vocation was landscape design. Vaux emphasized the creative freedom they would have under Stranahan and predicted that Prospect Park would be even more successful than Central Park.

Olmsted finally agreed, undoubtedly swayed by Mariposa's demise in 1865. It was a turning point in his life, and he would go on to become a towering figure in landscape architecture, designing magnificent parks around the country. He also became a city planner, developing suburban communities like Riverside, Illinois (with Vaux), and channeling urban growth through such devices as landscaped parkways.

Today we know a great deal about Olmsted, who authored an extraordinary collection of books, letters, and documents, including reports on the planning and construction of Prospect Park. (Vaux, on the other hand, left little of his legacy in print.) For a century, through a series of firms established and run by either Olmsted, his son Frederick Law Olmsted Jr., and his stepson, John Charles Olmsted, the Olmsteds would be involved in more than six thousand landscape architecture projects nationwide, ranging from private estates and suburban communities to public parks and academic campuses.

Nevertheless, Olmsted was nearly forgotten until the 1960s and early 1970s, when growing public awareness of environmental and preservation issues coincided with the 150th anniversary of his birth. He became the subject of coordinated exhibits at the Whitney Museum and at the National Gallery of Art, in which he was hailed as a visionary designer and an early environmentalist. The 1972 exhibits drew from forty-two thousand items found in various archives and museums, including the Library of Congress. The appearance of a number of books and dozens of articles about Olmsted's life and works coincided with the shows; the later publication of a multi-volume collection of his papers offered a treasure trove of information for students and historians.[34] The economic downturn in New York City during the 1970s also elevated Olmsted's reputation as public attention turned to the deteriorating Prospect and Central Parks and the need to restore them to their former grandeur.

The origins of Olmsted's personality and later success lie in his offbeat childhood and adolescence. He was born in 1822 in Hartford, Connecticut, the son of a well-to-do dry-goods merchant, John Olmsted. Some of Olmsted's earliest memories were of horseback rides and travels with his father through the New England countryside, where he learned to appreciate nature's untouched wonders. Charlotte Olmsted, his mother, died when he was three, and Olmsted's father married Mary Ann Bull, a close family friend, fourteen months later. John and Mary Ann began their own family and young Olmsted, being a somewhat difficult child, was sent away to school at seven years old to be tutored by clergymen—some caring, others frightful— until he was fifteen. This upbringing was totally different from Vaux's tightly structured education and environment. Connecticut was mostly wilderness. London was a crowded and gloomy metropolis of a million people. The contrast between the two experiences and their potential influences is intriguing: one can imagine Olmsted's hand in the curving, wide expanse of Long Meadow, see his passion for earth and trees, while Vaux would design the rustic shelters and the cozy warmth of the Dairy cottage, snug in Prospect Park's Ravine, with its dark, winding paths reminiscent of London's narrow streets.

Olmsted rambled about the countryside while at home and at school, leading "a decently restrained vagabond life."[35] His mind became a cauldron of unbridled curiosity; he read voraciously and developed a quick and keenly observant intellect. He was fiercely independent, restless, and strong-willed. Olmsted declined to attend Yale University in 1837, claiming ill health, but it might also have been because he was too undisciplined to submit to formal instruction.

Olmsted's character was quintessentially American—exuberant, outgoing, and rough and ready—while Vaux displayed typical English reserve. As a young man, Olmsted liked to spend time with friends in convivial, raucous gatherings until dawn, while Vaux preferred quiet, intellectual soirees. The American threw himself fully into every endeavor and often drove himself to exhaustion. His friend, George Templeton Strong, detected an inner turmoil that propelled the energetic young man: "When Olmsted is blue, the logic of his despondency is crushing and terrible."[36] When Olmsted later directed the United States Sanitary Commission during the Civil War, his friend observed that he "works like a dog all day and sits up nearly all night, doesn't go home to his family for five days and nights, works with steady, feverish intensity till four in the morning, sleeps on a sofa in his clothes, and breakfasts on strong coffee and pickles."[37] Late in life, Olmsted told a biographer that he questioned his life of "doing" rather than "being."[38]

The landscape designer is described by Olmsted biographer Witold Rybczynski as "dashing" and seen elegantly dressed with a cape hung nonchalantly over his shoulders in a historical photograph.[39] If not traditionally handsome, his face—with its broad forehead, widely separated and slightly hooded eyes, and sensitive mouth—attracted interest. During his youth his crown carried thick, curly dark hair that sometimes fell over his forehead and extended in the back to touch the top of his jacket collar. As a young man, photographs show him as clean-shaven except for a billowing mustache.

Instead of following his brother to Yale, Olmsted traveled and took on a host of jobs better suited to his temperament until well into his thirties, thanks to the financial support of his ever-indulging father. At fifteen he became an apprentice surveyor and learned to calculate how much earth was needed to reshape the land, how to lay out roads, and how to read and sketch topographical maps. He gained knowledge that would be useful years later when he would work on Central and Prospect Parks.

Tired of surveying, Olmsted moved to New York City to clerk at Benkard and Hutton, a dry-goods and silk-import business. He took a room in Mrs. Howard's boarding house on Henry Street in Brooklyn

Olmsted designed his parks to be rural escapes from the bustle of city life.

and commuted daily by ferry to Manhattan. Reacting to the clamor and uproar of mercantile New York, Olmsted longed for the distant countryside. In a letter to his stepmother, he described his yearning to return to nature:

Oh, how I long to be where I was a year ago: midst two lofty mountains, pursuing the uneven course of the purling brook, gliding among the fair granite rocks...meandering through the lowly valley, under the sweeping willows, & waving elms, where nought is heard save the indistinct clank of anvils & the distant roaring of water as it passes gracefully over the half natural dam of the beautiful Farmington.[40]

A year later, in 1843, the young adventurer signed up as a seaman on the *Ronaldson*, a ship sailing to China. Sea travel was something of a rite of passage in his day: it was in 1841 that Herman Melville voyaged on the whaling vessel *Acushnet*, as he would relate ten years later in *Moby Dick*. Richard Henry Dana likewise chronicled his time on the ocean in his book *Two Years before the Mast* (1840), which may have inspired Olmsted to take the voyage. Once on board the *Ronaldson*, he suffered from seasickness for weeks. When he recovered, he worked as a deckhand, "scrubbing, scraping and painting," but he was soon toiling on the riggings one hundred feet above the pitching deck. He experienced bad falls, endured a strange paralysis in his right arm, and like the rest of the crew grew weary of the monotonous food. After a year at sea, an exhausted and malnourished Olmsted returned to New York City.

Olmsted began studying farming shortly thereafter, and for the next seven years, he made a living as a farmer, first on land in Connecticut purchased by his father and then on his 123-acre Tosomock Farm on Staten Island. Here he gained further insight into horticulture by learning soil-management techniques—in particular, the benefits of proper drainage. He also developed a small commercial nursery and acquired knowledge about trees that he would apply at Prospect Park, where he later managed the planting of thousands of seedlings and hundreds of mature trees.

In 1850—the same year that Vaux arrived in the United States—Olmsted set off to explore England with his brother John and his friend Charles Loring Brace, a theology student. Although principally a trip to study farming techniques, it also satisfied Olmsted's adventurous spirit, serving as a milestone and introducing him to the sublimity of the English countryside. They landed in Liverpool and crossed the Mersey River to Birkenhead, which, like Brooklyn, was a rapidly developing suburb dependent on a neighboring city's port. Birkenhead was the site of a new park designed by John Paxton, later known for his work at Chatsworth, an extravagant estate surrounded by expansive parkland, and for the Crystal Palace in London.

Birkenhead Park's 120 acres consisted of meadows, woods, ponds, and winding paths and carriage drives. Visitors could stroll, play cricket, or practice archery. Olmsted noticed the park's details, absorbed them, and recorded them all in letters, articles, and

Olmsted was smitten by the beauty of the English countryside with its sheep and patchwork fields, as seen in this picture of the Wye Valley.

notebooks. He reported that in England, where most open spaces were the hunting reserves and estates of the aristocracy, Birkenhead was the first government-funded people's park where "the poorest British peasant is free to enjoy it in all of its parts as the British Queen.... I was ready to admit that in democratic America there was nothing to be thought as comparable with this People's Garden."[41]

The 1,193-acre private park at Eaton Hall, one of the seats of the Marquis of Westminster, Lord High Chamberlain to Queen Victoria, was another favorite destination. "Ah! Here is a real park at last," Olmsted wrote. "A gracefully, irregular, gently undulating surface of close cropped pasture land, reaching way off illimitably; dark green in colour: very old, but not very large trees scattered singly and in groups—so far apart as to throw long unbroken shadows across broad openings of light."[42] He couldn't help point out, though, that it—unlike Birkenhead—was a private reserve.

When Olmsted returned to the United States, he authored a book on his experiences, *Walks and Talks of an American Farmer in England*, and published an article on Birkenhead Park in the *Horticulturist*.[43] In 1853 he traveled through parts of the American South and later wrote about southern society and slavery in the *New York Daily Times* as well as in books, such as in his work *A Journey Through Texas*, published in 1857. With these writings Olmsted established his voice as an authoritative commentator on not only nature and the environment but also contemporary politics and culture. His treatises on slavery influenced the abolitionist platform of the newly formed Republican Party that would nominate Lincoln for president.

In 1855 he became the managing editor of *Putnam's Monthly Magazine*, a leading literary journal that included political commentary. Through the magazine he became acquainted with many of the most respected literary figures and social philosophers of the day, including Henry Wadsworth Longfellow, James Russell Lowell, Harriet Beecher Stowe, Washington Irving, and William Thackeray.

The social critic and writer Lewis Mumford referred to Olmsted's prolonged apprenticeship as "American education at its best."[44] Olmsted's travels, personal and professional associations, and love of reading, Mumford explained, exposed him to the forces of his age and the social and intellectual theories expounded by social reformers and naturalists. Olmsted had witnessed the inequities and struggles of many—the plight of the American slaves, the poverty of the British working class, the oppression of lowly seamen, and the conditions of immigrants in rapidly expanding cities. He came to believe that public parks were a refuge, however small, where the common man could feel a sense of ownership.

When *Putnam's* failed, Olmsted was at a crossroads and realized that he could no longer turn to his father for support as he had for years. In 1859 he married Mary Perkins Olmsted, the widow of his brother John, who had died in 1858 of tuberculosis. Olmsted was now stepfather to three children he needed to support. He had four children of his own with Mary, two of whom—a son and a daughter—survived to adulthood.

A short time before, in 1857, New York City's Park Commission approved Viele's plan for what would eventually become Central Park and had begun construction but needed a superintendent who would oversee the work. Olmsted jumped at the chance and persuaded James Hamilton, son of Alexander Hamilton, and other influential New Yorkers to help him secure the position. He touted his knowledge of soil and the administrative skills he gained from managing farmhands. His efforts were fruitful, and in September 1857 he was offered the job—more likely due to his forceful personality and social connections than his experience.

With his usual single-minded determination, Olmsted supervised a workforce of hundreds of men under Chief Engineer Viele. Meanwhile Vaux, now living and practicing in New York, called Viele's plan for the new park "outrageous" and a "disgrace" that maligned Downing's memory. When the Park Commission held a competition for a redesign of the park's landscape in 1857, Vaux turned to Olmsted for assistance, counting on Olmsted's experience as superintendent for the park's construction, and his knowledge of the park's layout, soil conditions, and engineering requirements. Vaux had read *Walks and Talks of an American Farmer in England* and was impressed by Olmsted's interest in and appreciation of landscape design. Their winning plan for Central Park, called the Greensward Plan—*greensward* is an English term referring to a long, unbroken expanse of grass—has been described as "a brilliant solution": it transformed 843 acres of rock outcroppings, barren ground, and swamp into a masterpiece of natural-looking landscape shaped and melded by imagination. Construction was well underway in 1861 when the Civil War erupted.[45]

With the building of Central Park at a standstill, Olmsted left to head the United States Sanitary Commission. He could not enlist in the military because a carriage accident in 1860 had left him with a permanent limp. As the general secretary of the sanitary commission, he was responsible for monitoring the medical condition of the Union army soldiers and for establishing facilities to care for the wounded and the sick. His work took him close to the battlefield, and he recorded in letters to friends the horror of war during the Peninsular Campaign of 1862:

> *Wounded were arriving by every train, entirely unattended.... They were packed as closely as they could be stowed in the common freight cars, without beds, without straw, at most with a wisp of hay under their heads. They arrived, dead and alive together, in the same close box, many with awful wounds festering and alive with maggots. The stench was such as to produce vomiting with some of our strong men, habituated to the duty of attending the sick & wounded of the army.*[46]

Physical and emotional exhaustion compelled Olmsted to resign from his position in 1864. It was then that he moved his family to California to direct the Mariposa Mining Estate. A year later he received Vaux's request for him to return to New York City to design

Prospect Park. There is a dearth of written correspondence between the two men, particularly during the construction of Prospect Park, suggesting a close and fruitful partnership in which they likely solved issues verbally. One could imagine Prospect Park as the product of a perfect collaboration between two partners at the peak of their abilities, an alliance so effective that neither man was ever as creative as when they worked together here. The design for the park became a template upon which many great future parks were based, including their own designs for Riverside and Morningside Parks in New York as well as Chicago's South Park and the park system in Buffalo, New York.

Olmsted, however, would soon eclipse his partner as he applied that model to many other projects around the country and became the nation's leading landscape architect. During the years after Prospect Park opened, Olmsted was involved in the development of parks in Montreal; Bridgeport, Connecticut; Rochester, New York; Wilmington, Delaware; Baltimore; Detroit; Milwaukee; Boston; and Chicago. He designed the grounds surrounding the United States Capitol, the landscape at the Biltmore, the Vanderbilt estate in North Carolina, and, two years before his retirement, the grounds for the World's Columbian Exposition of 1893 in Chicago. Despite the many parks that Olmsted worked on after his association with Vaux, Prospect Park remained his finest accomplishment.

The portrait artist John Singer Sargent's 1895 painting of Olmsted depicts him in old age, as a man with a flowing white beard leaning on a cane and looking on the world with limpid, sympathetic eyes. Time was not kind to Olmsted: he suffered from dementia and, in 1898, was confined by his wife to the McLean Asylum in Waverly, Massachusetts—where he had designed the landscape. The old guard was slipping away: Stranahan died in 1898, three years after Vaux, and Olmsted died at McLean in 1903 amid the very features he had shaped: palettes of light and shadow, stands of lofty oaks and hickories, and textured rolling meadows.

Chapter Three

THE OLMSTED AND VAUX PLAN

N 1865 PROSPECT PARK WAS NOT QUITE A BLANK canvas, but it was close. Olmsted and Vaux were handed a largely barren and unfruitful plot on which to create the landscape they imagined. Olmsted described their vision in an 1866 report to the Brooklyn Park Commission:

Although we cannot have wild mountain gorges, for instance, on the park, we may have rugged ravines shaded with trees and made picturesque with shrubs, the forms and arrangement of which remind us of mountain scenery. We may perhaps even secure some slight approach to the mystery, variety and luxuriance of tropical scenery, by an assemblage of certain forms of vegetation, gay with flow-ers, and intricate and mazy with vines and creepers, ferns, rushes and broad leaved plants. [1]

Inspiration and Main Elements

Prospect Park reflects many features of the English landscape and parks, especially Birkenhead Park. Vaux and Olmsted favored the work of the great landscape architects and gardeners of eighteenth-century Britain, whose designs were a radical departure from the formally planted gardens previously popular in Europe. Vaux grew up surrounded by this beauty while Olmsted returned twice to Birkenhead after his first visit there in 1850 and met with gardeners, landscape architects, and engineers. He revisited Birkenhead in 1859 and again in 1878, to obtain the "full particulars of its construction, maintenance and management." [2]

A nineteenth-century Birkenhead map reveals remarkable simi-larities to Prospect Park. Both are somewhat diamond-shaped, have perimeter drives that encircle interior meadows and wooded copses, and are graced by a lake at the south end. Birkenhead was also fash-ioned from wasteland—a flat, sterile, clay farm—and the ground was thoroughly underdrained, as was the case at Prospect Park. The earth dredged from Birkenhead's lake was used to shape the undulating meadows. Boulders and rocks not needed for the drives were laid in groups, and ferns and moss were planted on them. In his book *Walks and Talks of an American Farmer in England*, Olmsted described his exploration of Birkenhead with an air of romance:

We [Olmsted and his companions] passed by winding paths, over acres and acres, with a constant varying surface, where on all sides were growing every variety of shrubs and flowers, with more than natural grace....We came to an open field of clean, bright, greensward, closely mown....Beyond this was a large meadow with rich groups of trees, under which a flock of sheep were reposing. [3]

Birkenhead and England etched themselves deeply into Olmsted's mind. "Such a country!" he wrote in his classic style, "Green, dripping, glistening, gorgeous! We stood dumbstricken by its loveliness...the

mild sun beaming through the watery atmosphere and all so quiet—
the hum of the bees and the crisp grass…but there we were right
in the midst of it; long time silent and then speaking softly as if it were
enchantment indeed, we gazed upon it and breathed it—never to be
forgotten.[4]

Similarly to Birkenhead, the three basic elements Olmsted and
Vaux used in their design for Prospect Park—meadow, wood, and
water—were separated to create different experiences, yet they were
harmoniously linked to generate a sense of space, unending distance,
and seclusion from the chaos of a large city. The impression of nature
was important. One would enter the park through archways punched
into the encircling berm, which was concealed by dense vegetation and
thick bushes, to encounter the ninety-acre Long Meadow that seemed
to stretch on forever. The bogs of peat left over from the ice age were
to be filled, small knolls added, and mounds that obstructed views
diminished. The cleared ground would become a great undulating
lawn fit for an English estate. Almost a mile in length, the Long Meadow
would wander and turn, making it appear limitless. Bordering trees
would be planted, both singly and in groups, casting long shadows that
would add visual depth and interest. Sheep and cows scattered throughout would offer a sense of scale and introduce animal life. All of these
features would continually draw the visitors into and through the park.

The park's Ravine, carved by nature and man from the Harbor
Hill moraine, would have a dense and carefully planted understory,

OVERLEAF
The design that Olmsted and Vaux
submitted to the Park Commission
shows the separation and
interweaving of water, woods,
and meadow.

PROSPECT PARK

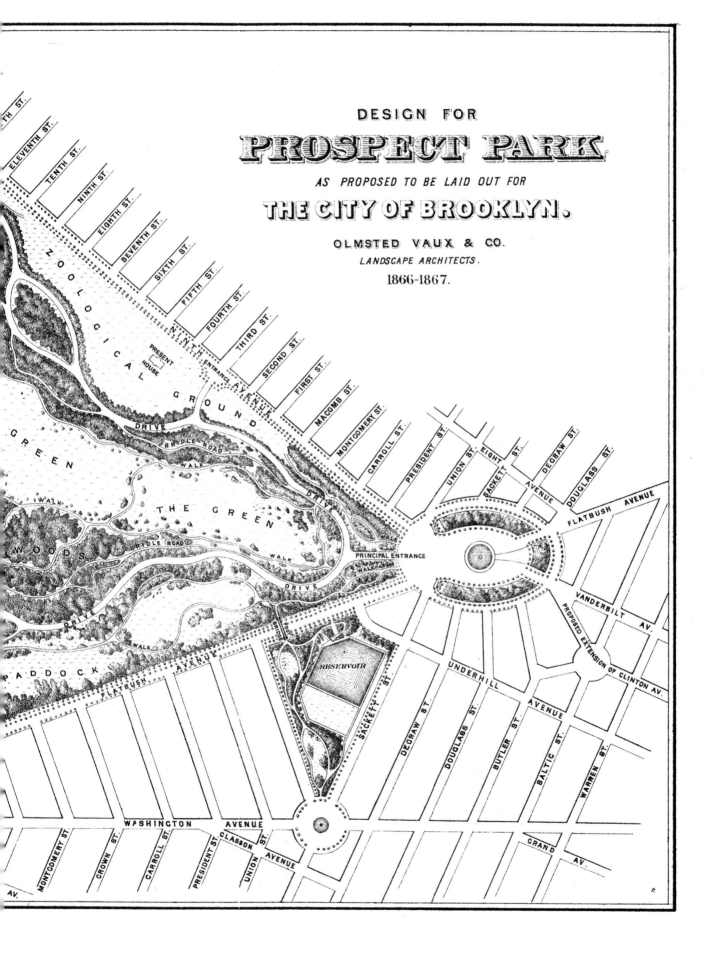

DESIGN FOR

PROSPECT PARK.

AS PROPOSED TO BE LAID OUT FOR

THE CITY OF BROOKLYN.

OLMSTED VAUX & CO.

LANDSCAPE ARCHITECTS.

1866-1867.

PROSPECT PARK

The Long Meadow in winter
offers a solitary splendor away
from the clamor of the city.

PROSPECT PARK

heavily textured and varying in color and form. Towering canopies of oak, chestnut, and hickory trees would provide shade and a reprieve from even the hottest day, and this part of the park would be transformed into a secret garden of paths twisting through a landscape of steep chasms and forests dappled in shade. The line of sight was to be purposely obscured by a maze of ridges, and a turn here and there would lead deeper into a tantalizing unknown. Visitors would lose their sense of direction in this illusion of Adirondacks wilderness. A gravity-fed watercourse would be excavated to create a rippling brook that flows over falls and into quiet ponds, descending seventy-six feet from beginning to end. The sounds of water over falls and weirs and around stones would draw visitors deeper into the woods, where the silence would be occasionally broken by the shriek of a hawk and the squawk and trill of the red-winged blackbird.

OPPOSITE, TOP
Tree canopies weave intricate patterns in the park.

OPPOSITE, BOTTOM
Light snow covers the Long Meadow near a stand of Turkey oaks.

LEFT
The sound of water in nature is an important element in Olmsted and Vaux's landscapes. Prospect Park has many small waterfalls, and one often hears the rush of the tumbling stream before it comes into view.

BELOW
In winter the path of the Ambergill, the park's man-made stream, is more clearly seen.

Olmsted and Vaux designed the Lake to capture the reflection of Lookout Hill.

In winter the Ravine would appear brown and black, its ridges exposed and icy, its brooks and falls frozen white. In summer it would be deeply shaded, the darkness breaking as one walked through an arch to a sunlit meadowlike clearing, the Nethermead. The stream would slow as it moved to the Lullwater—deeper, calmer, wider, quilted with water lilies, patrolled by waterfowl, and hemmed by foliage—and then it would flow imperceptibly into the sixty-acre Lake, with its meandering shoreline and tiny islands abundant with wildlife, bulrushes, and cattails. Boaters could drift for hours, and pedestrians could follow footpaths along the four-mile shore and never see the edges of the park. They might pause at rough-hewn rustic shelters offering views of the Lake, reflecting gold at sunrise or sunset, sparkling in the noonday sun, and gleaming like basalt in the black of night. In the winter a tableau of hundreds of skaters would cover the Lake.

A wily Vaux read James Stranahan's mind when he proposed the Lake and included it in his 1865 plan that extended Viele's proposed park by 228 acres to the south. The new land added more wood-lands and also comprised the Nethermead, Lookout Hill, the Quaker (Friends) Cemetery—which is still owned and used today by the Quakers—and an extension of the Long Meadow to Fifteenth Street. The Lake, Vaux told Stranahan, would be more than twice the size of its counterpart in Central Park, and the "wizard" of Brooklyn was delighted with this further proof that Prospect Park would be better than Central Park.

Vistas were essential elements in the fabric of Prospect Park. In the 1860s the crests of the Ravine and Breeze and Lookout Hills offered panoramic views in all directions, toward New Jersey's Watchung Hills, beyond the Narrows to the Atlantic Ocean, and to New York City, where church spires and ships' masts were the tallest structures. Olmsted and Vaux planned a terraced platform on Lookout Hill with seats and awnings connected to an oval carriage court by a broad terrace walk and staircase. Breeze Hill was later the site of Camera Obscura, built in 1874—a boxlike, enclosed theater where visitors could marvel at landscape scenes, the Lullwater, the Lake, and the distant views, all projected from an overhead lens onto a circular white tabletop. A footbridge was proposed from the park over Flatbush Avenue to the summit of Mount Prospect, where the views were even more impressive.

Views within the park were equally important. Artfully planted stands of trees dotted the landscape to draw the attention of visitors, and the view of the Long Meadow appeared and disappeared behind foliage, tantalizing carriage riders as they passed by. The drives, walkways, and bridle paths were designed to dip and rise to offer dynamic views. The entrance arches not only framed the landscape but also highlighted the moods and scenes that changed with the seasons. Even the time of day made a difference, as the shadows constantly shifted.

It was through the employment of these design elements—tricks, if you will—that Olmsted and Vaux sought to create a powerful contrast to the clamoring city streets. Significantly, in the 1866 report to the Park Commission, the designers quoted the Twenty-third Psalm: "He maketh me to lie down in green pastures; He leadeth me beside the still waters."[5]

The views from Lookout Hill were prized in the late nineteenth century. Midtown Manhattan is what you can see from the hill today, if you are raised seventy-five feet in a bucket truck.

OVERLEAF
An American elm shows its exquisite design throughout the seasons on the Long Meadow.

OPPOSITE
Unlike the city street grid pattern,
the park's drives and paths are
never straight.

ABOVE
The seasonal colors and the
interplay of light and shadows are
what make the park a continuously
compelling visual experience.

East Side Lands

The Olmsted and Vaux plan excluded most of the land on the east side of Flatbush Avenue, known as the East Side Lands, that Viele had included in his proposal. They did, however, set aside the ground around the Prospect Hill Reservoir—today's Mount Prospect Park—for a promenade that would wind its way up to the summit and offer spectacular views.

Olmsted and Vaux had learned from their experience in Central Park that a park was not inviolate: many groups wished to build facilities of one kind or another within its boundaries. Therefore, they recommended to the city officials that a portion of the East Side Lands that abutted Flatbush Avenue be held for institutions, such as museums and libraries. Stranahan liked this plan and calculated that the East Side Lands could be sold to pay for the additional acreage to the south for the Lake. But not everyone agreed and the issue was controversial for twenty years. Some factions wanted the East Side Lands included in the park, while others, including many former landowners whose land had been taken by the city for the future park, wanted their properties returned at enhanced values. The courts ruled in favor of the commission, which spent hundreds of thousands of dollars improving the land for eventual sale by subdividing it and adding sewer and water services. Because of the economic panic of the 1870s, the land was not sold until 1888.

Bringing People Together

There were social objectives inherent in the design of Prospect Park. "Men must come together," Olmsted wrote, "and must be seen coming together, in carriages, on horseback and on foot and the concourse of animated life which will thus be formed, must in itself be made, if possible, an attractive and diverting spectacle." The park was to appeal to the rich but also to the working class and poor; rich and poor alike were to see and be seen. Olmsted and Vaux hoped that Brooklynites of different backgrounds would find a common ground in the park and engage with each other, "unembarrassed by limitations that surround them at home."[6] Prospect Park would belong to everyone.

The Lake would be the center of this interaction. Drives and footpaths led to Lookout Hill, where, on the terrace, visitors could congregate, take in fresh breezes and distant panoramas, and have

LEFT
The view from the Concert Grove toward Music Island in 1930

RIGHT
Tear Drop Island from the Concert Grove, c. 1910

Berms surround much of
the park to define the landscape
within and separate it from
the city without.

a grandstand view of military drills taking place on the Parade Ground. The Concert Grove and Music Island formed an area where visitors could come to listen to concerts performed for audiences as large as ten thousand—some seated in the shade, some in their equipages on the nearby carriage concourse, and others up on Breeze Hill.

Vaux also drafted plans for an elegant restaurant called the Refectory—situated between the Concert Grove and Lookout Hill in a crook along the shore where the Lullwater meets the Lake—which he hoped would be a popular destination. Lookout Hill, the Concert Grove, and Music Island were linked by a promenade and a concourse fashioned from a flaring of the drive and walkway. The promenade was more than a pedestrian avenue, providing a venue where classes and communities could mingle. Promenading had become a widespread cultural and social custom in the United States and in Europe during the nineteenth century, furthering the designers' belief that parks could have a democratizing and civilizing influence. When the park closed at night, in fact, people would continue to promenade on the sidewalks—lined with evergreens and lit by gas lamps—ringing the outside boundary of the park.

Drives, Paths, and Walkways

Threading through the park and binding it were five miles of drives, four miles of bridle paths, and twenty miles of walkways. The meandering drives framed the park, while the bridle paths generally paralleled them but also branched into the Ravine. The walks wound throughout most of the park—there were no straight lines—creating the impression of unending space. Walkways bisected and followed the perimeter of the Long Meadow, passed through the Ravine, and wrapped around the Lake to the top of Lookout Hill. Five arches in the perimeter berm offered safe entries to the pedestrians, points where they could pass without crossing the path of a carriage or horse.

The twenty-foot-high berm surrounding much of the park defined it and separated it from the city, and provided an impenetrable screen to block the sights and sounds of encroaching development. The outer

PREVIOUS
The western woods create
an additional buffer against
the city and are a world
unto themselves.

areas of the park, which Olmsted and Vaux designated as the "perimeter," constituted 170 acres and included grounds for a zoo and a deer paddock. The Plaza was also included in the perimeter and was its most important feature. Later named Grand Army Plaza, it has come to symbolize the grandeur of Prospect Park. The original design, consisting of an oval-shaped commons separated from additional traffic by high berms, broke up the city's street grid plan.

The West Lands

The park's perimeter was expanded in 1869 with the addition of a strip along Prospect Park West, then called Ninth Avenue. Known as the West Lands, the new land came at a cost of $1.7 million (land speculation around the park had increased real estate values). The parcel—which Vaux called the "Expensive Lands"—included property previously owned by Brooklyn Democrat political boss Hugh McLaughlin as well as the sumptuous Litchfield Villa, designed by the architect Alexander Jackson Davis, known for his elegant country houses.

Litchfield Villa was built in 1857 for Edwin Clark Litchfield, a lawyer and railroad financier. He owned property stretching from the villa to the Gowanus Canal, which he developed as a shipping channel. Standing atop a knoll in what was then called Greenwood Heights, Litchfield Villa offered sweeping views from Lower Manhattan to the Atlantic Ocean. Italianate in style, the building's

ABOVE
Litchfield Villa, c. 1890s. Edwin Clark
Litchfield's mansion, constructed
in 1857, was originally called Grace
Hill after Litchfield's wife.

RIGHT
A path to the Long Meadow
seen from a back window of
Litchfield Villa

exterior was stucco painted and scored to imitate stone. The man–sion included square towers, rounded turrets, balconies, and a large three-story entrance hall, which was decorated with English Minton tiles and capped with a central skylight. Litchfield named the mansion Grace Hill after his wife, Grace Hill Hubbard, and leased the property back from the Park Commission from 1869 until 1883. Today Litchfield Villa houses the offices of the Prospect Park admin-istration and the Brooklyn headquarters of the New York City Department of Parks and Recreation.

The Parade Ground

A parade ground, an important feature in most American commu-nities at the time, was not included in Olmsted and Vaux's original planning report but was later added on forty adjacent acres at the park's south end. In the 1870s there was no professional army to speak of, but the local or state militia needed grounds for close-order drills. Almost immediately after its opening in 1867, various regiments of the New York National Guard began to practice on the Parade Ground. A chalet-style lodge and shelter designed by Vaux was erected on the ground's western edge and contained a guardroom, bathrooms, an officials' room, and a public space. Much of the build-ing was devoted to a covered shelter with open bays, which was used by the spectators at military drills and parades.

The Parkways

In their 1866 plan for Prospect Park Olmsted and Vaux proposed the construction of three grand thoroughfares originating in the park. One was to be called Ravenswood, which would connect Prospect Park with the East River and Central Park via ferry, but it was never built. The construction of Ocean and Eastern Parkways, however, began in 1868. Eastern Parkway, initially named Jamaica Park Way in 1871, stretched two and a half miles to the east. Ocean Parkway, built over the Coney Island Plank Road, linked the park to Coney Island. The central section of both roads was a wide boulevard bordered by tree-lined walkways that separated adjoining service roads or bridle paths. The outer edges had additional sidewalks.

Olmsted and Vaux saw the boulevards as extensions of the park that conveyed a sense of being grand entryways to a great imperial city and would help advance the park's future growth and development. There was also a practical, political motivation behind the proposal for the boulevards: During the first half of the nineteenth century the people and leaders of Brooklyn could not decide between plans for one or two major parks. The compromise was to create a series of smaller parks connected by attractively designed parkways that were, in effect, parks themselves. Olmsted and Vaux would later achieve this concept more successfully in their park-system design for Buffalo, New York.

The idea of boulevards was not new: Berlin and Paris already had grand avenues connecting parks and public places, most famously the 1.2-mile-long Champs Elysées. Stretching from the Place de la Concorde to the Arc de Triomphe, the broad thoroughfare was—and still is—bordered by elegant walks and arching trees. Morris Reynolds, a Brooklyn businessman, is credited with suggesting, in 1859, that a central boulevard two hundred feet wide should connect Prospect Park with the Atlantic Ocean, with formal lines of trees, sidewalks, two carriage ways, and a middle section adaptable for possible street railway development. Reynolds referred to his proposal in the *Eagle* as "one of the most magnificent drives in the world."[7] The *Eagle* and the Park Commission enthusiastically supported the concept, and Stranahan strongly endorsed a similar system in 1861 in the commission's annual report: "Some earnestly advocated the adoption of a plan for a grand drive or carriage road, to extend from Fort Hamilton to Green Point, connecting a chain of five parks."[8]

Construction Begins

Olmsted and Vaux's 1866 park plan was modified somewhat in the five subsequent versions presented during the next eight years. Little was changed, however, besides place names: part of the Lake became Lullwater; the Green was renamed the Long Meadow; and the Deer Paddock, the Hart Range. The Zoological Ground disappeared in the 1869 version, and the Upper Pool and Parade Ground appeared in 1870. Despite the enormity of the task, once underway the project would develop much more smoothly than Olmsted and Vaux's more famous undertaking across the East River.

Prospect Park proved easier to build than Central Park. Its subsurface was softer and facilitated excavation. There was greater public support, and Olmsted and Vaux were not plagued by constant official interference as they had been with Central Park. Above all there was an experienced team of designers—Olmsted and Vaux—and engineers—C. C. Martin and John Y. Culyer—who had free reign to design and develop the park.

The design for Ocean Parkway, pictured here in 1896, incorporated the first bicycle path in the United States.

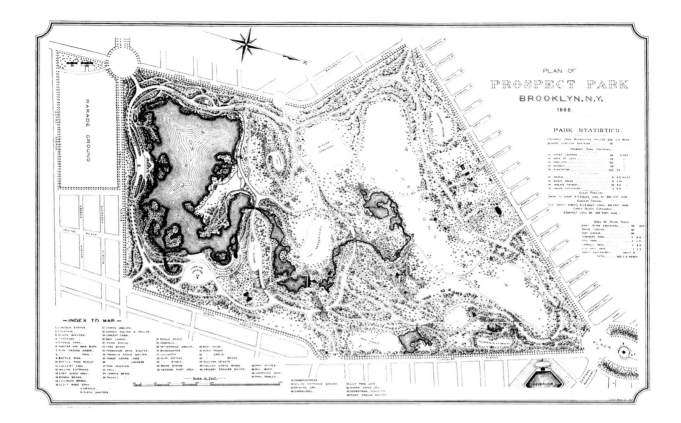

Construction began on July 1, 1866. Overnight the grounds became a major building site filled with the shouts of workers, the clanging and banging of tools, the clops of horses, and the occasional hiss and throb of a steam engine. The *Eagle* reported on the tumult: "Once inside the Park all is chaos. Carts rumble, dust flies, men delve and sweat, and the jolly foremen look lazily about to see that every laborer is doing his duty."[9]

It is difficult today to imagine what it would have been like to witness armies of workers building and shaping Prospect Park at the dawn of the machine age. Eighteen hundred men, using mostly picks and shovels, toiled at the site at one time or another; alongside them were scores of horses and mules. Many of the workers were immigrants new to Brooklyn and were organized into barrow gangs, cart gangs, stone-breaking gangs, and team gangs (for horses). Brick masons, stonemasons, carpenters, "rustic" carpenters, master gardeners, and blacksmiths were also a part of the workforce. In 1872 the park employed 1,351 unskilled and 55 skilled laborers and maintained 212 carts, 87 teams, and 193 mechanics. The workers were arranged in groups of twenty to fifty men; military-style roll calls were conducted three times a day. Eight men were employed exclusively for watch duty to ensure that the workmen kept to their jobs. The workday lasted ten hours. Stranahan was pleased that the park saved money by paying workers a daily wage of $1.70 compared to $2.00 for an eight-hour workday at Central Park.[10]

Today the available earth-moving equipment would grade Long Meadow and scoop out the Lake in short order. Cherry pickers would help prune trees, and power saws would dispatch dead ones. Dump

Olmsted and Vaux's 1866 park design went through several modifications. Shown here is the plan of 1888.

The park's original terrain was rocky, sometimes swampy farmland bordered by woods, as seen in this photograph of 1866.

trucks would haul away debris, move dirt quickly, and deposit it where it was needed. In 1866 wheelbarrows, horse-drawn carts, and a horse-drawn rail system did all this. Steam-powered machinery was just beginning to appear, and Prospect Park's engineers, always in favor of new technology, brought in an American-designed rock crusher and a steamroller from Liverpool, England, to build the park's roads and paths.

The Park's Drainage System

Most park visitors today are oblivious to the extent of the work that went into shaping Prospect Park. They may think that the major effort was in the shaping of the landscape and the selection of plantings, but what is underground is just as important as what is aboveground. The first order of business was, in fact, the introduction of a water drainage system that, to this day, branches out like an invisible web underneath the Long Meadow, portions of the Ravine, the Nethermead, and around the Lake. As at Central Park, Olmsted became something of a chief engineer at Prospect Park, overseeing the installation of vitrified—heat-tempered or chemically treated—clay drainpipes.

The mainstay of the system is two large sections of fifteen-inch pipes that lie beneath the length of the Long Meadow from the entrance of Grand Army Plaza to Fifteenth Street. These main lines are fed by a series of smaller pipes, with diameters from two to twelve inches, that spread across the meadow. Runoff flows from the smallest pipes, through a series of vaulted retention basins, into the largest pipes, before emptying into the waterways. Additional lines connected the Brooklyn Botanic Garden and East Drive to the Lake. The network was designed to absorb a maximum of two inches of rain per hour.

With his experience as a farmer, Olmsted knew that saturated ground was unsuitable for vegetation, and he had carefully studied the drainage at Birkenhead Park. "The whole ground," he wrote of Birkenhead, "was thoroughly under-drained, the minor drains of stone, the main of tile."[11] One of his first assignments at Central Park was to create a drainage system; the same was required of him at Prospect Park.

Olmsted was well ahead of his time in recognizing the importance of drainage in parks and the benefits of capturing runoff to fill the waterways and lakes. Today it is a topic that not only concerns parks but also towns and cities countrywide. The prevailing method used in many cities has been to direct runoff into the municipal sewer system, which overtaxes wastewater treatment plants. It makes much more environmental and economical sense to use runoff to replenish public bodies of water, as was the case at Prospect Park.

Shaping the Park

Olmsted developed extensive topographical maps of the park that the workers carefully followed to create the desired landscaping effect. The grades and lines of the drives, bridge-roads, and walks; the terrain and the inclines of the slopes, meadows, and concourses;

as well as the heights of the fillings and the depths of the excavations were determined through use of these maps.

The shaping of the Long Meadow began at the north end, near the Plaza and the Endale and Meadowport Arches, where thirty thousand cubic yards of peat was removed. Workers filled in the kettle ponds and peat bogs with rich farm soil excavated from the Lake mixed with horse manure, night soil (human waste), lime, and fish guano. Some glacial mounds were reduced, others were enhanced; an existing series of embankments on the west side that had been built for a future street system was removed, and the earthen perimeter berm was added. The walkways at the Long Meadow were recessed to provide an unobstructed view across its length and to magnify the sense of distance. The drives and walkways were often built on elevated ground to accentuate the views.

Much of the forested portions of the Midwood, the Ravine, along the East Drive, and Lookout and Breeze Hills had deteriorated from years of neglect. The soil was unfertile, and trees and shrubs were languishing. New soil was added, and the dead trees were uprooted. Those that could be saved were pruned, and thousands of new trees were sown and existing trees transplanted with great care to create a sense of openness and to soften the contrast between the old woods and the new. In 1869, 43,292 trees and shrubs were planted and another 107,688 young trees and shrubs were being raised in the park's nursery. An *Eagle* reporter marveled at the plantings in 1871:

> *Every tree is a thick, leafy covert, and rare shrubs, which had been imported at a great expense from Europe, have taken root, and are thriving in a manner that has surprised the most experienced gardeners. Many of them are planted in groups but they have spread themselves with such unlooked for luxuriance that transplanting has had to be resorted to in order to give each plant sufficient room in which to do itself justice.…The transplanting of large trees has also been carried on with great success, and some of the finest looking trees in the park are those which have been carted around from one place to another.*[12]

John Y. Culyer's tree-moving machine made transplanting large trees easier.

A park gardener designed this extension ladder for tree pruning.

Large trees with root balls weighing up to fifteen tons and measuring five feet in circumference were regularly transplanted from within the park and others donated from outside. Culyer designed two large, horse-drawn "tree-moving machines" for the purpose, wooden wagons with spoked wooden wheels nearly as tall as a man. In one year six hundred trees weighing one ton or more were relocated using these machines. The gardening foreman also developed a pruning ladder with extensions to reach the tallest trees.

One wonders how the Ravine with its brook, waterfalls, steep ridges, and boulders was constructed without the benefit of modern earth-moving machinery. Many of the boulders used to build the Fallkill and Ambergill waterfalls weighed several tons, yet these ice-age erratics were hoisted into precise positions, one on top of the other, with nothing more than a basic understanding of physics and the muscle power of man and beast. Under Olmsted's supervision, men dug the Ravine's waterways; reshaped its slopes; excavated the Upper Pool, the Lower Pool, the Lullwater, and the Lake with picks and shovels; and removed the earth with barrows and horse carts.

Excavation of the Lake, started in 1867, was the largest construction project in Prospect Park and proceeded in stages. A five-acre area was dammed off in 1868 for a temporary pond that drew two hundred thousand skaters from January to March, and by 1871 a thirty-acre section nearest the Lullwater was completed. So much earth was removed during construction of the Lake, which reaches down seven feet at its deepest point, that workers built a portable horse-drawn railroad to haul topsoil from this onetime vegetable field and use it to fill in other parts of the park.

Problems at the Lake arose immediately: five thousand gallons of water evaporated daily in hot weather, and the porous clay liner leaked. The clay, a by-product of the glacial age, was extracted from abundant deposits near the Deer Paddock and laid down on the lake bed using a process called puddling, in which the clay was mixed with water to form a paste and spread across the surface. The solution to the seepage was to allow silt to create a seal. This liner is in place to this day.

The Well

A well at the base of Lookout Hill was built to feed the pools and the waterways that flowed into the Lake. The project was supervised by Martin, who was the chief engineer at the start of the park's construction. Martin was a "cool and unruffled" civil-engineering graduate (from Rensselaer Polytechnic Institute in Troy, New York), with experience in building numerous bridges as well as the Atlantic Dock and the Brooklyn water system.[13]

His well was a technological achievement and probably the most complicated construction and engineering project undertaken at Prospect Park. It too was the product of hand labor. To construct the well, Martin built a large cylinder fifty-four feet in diameter, made of cast iron and wood and held together by iron rods. The cylinder was lowered inch by inch as workers dug out the soil,

rock, and sand to a depth of seventy feet, the level of the water table. Debris was hoisted out in a steam-powered bucket, and masons erected a thick layer of bricks around the inner cylinder wall. By some accounts the well was then the world's largest and provided Martin with a dry run for the caissons that would support the Brooklyn Bridge, for which he was the chief engineer. The well attracted so many gawking visitors that the walkway to the adjacent Well and Boiler House was replaced with a drive and the wooden footbridge across the Lullwater with the iron-clad Terrace Bridge to accommodate the tourists' carriages.

The Well and Boiler House, designed by Vaux of Croton brick trimmed with Ohio stone, housed a coal-powered steam engine that pumped well water through pipes to a 750,000-gallon underground

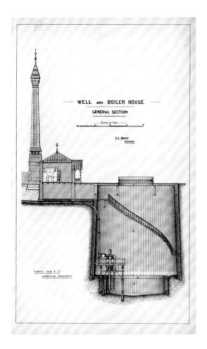

reservoir on the summit of Lookout Hill. The reservoir was twelve feet deep and covered with a roof supported by brick arches that became the foundation of the Lookout Hill pedestrian concourse. Water flowed through pipes from the reservoir to the Fallkill waterfall.

Initially, the well provided the park with an annual supply of 164 million gallons of water, but in 1889 it was deepened to accommodate the needs of new lawn tennis courts and the profusion of ornamental flower gardens. Demand increased so dramatically that the Park Commission eventually turned to the city to provide water, and today the system can be turned on and off almost as easily as a kitchen faucet. Accordingly, the Well and Boiler House and reservoir became redundant, and while the Well and Boiler House remains and will be converted to restrooms, the reservoir was filled in during the 1930s.

Construction of the Drives and Walks

The building of the drives provides additional insight into mid-nineteenth-century construction techniques and methods. They were made of stone blocks—called Telford blocks—and stone rubble mined on site. A steam-powered Blake stone breaker produced gravel of varying sizes and saved hours of labor that would otherwise have been done by hand with a sledge and hammer. The roadbeds were dug to a depth of twenty-seven inches and overlaid with a thick course of sand. The imported steamroller, first used in the park in August of 1869, operated day and night and compacted the newly built drives with great efficiency. The machine cost ten dollars a day to operate and rolled twice the amount of surface as the seven-ton roller hauled by an eight-horse team that cost twenty dollars a day. It also moved backward, whereas the horse team had to be turned around to complete multiple passes.

The seven-inch-thick Telford blocks forming the drives' surface were laid directly over the sand. The base of each wedge-shaped block

faced down, and the cavities at the top were filled with spalls—stone chips—hammered into place to create a rigid and smooth surface. The surfaces were crowned so that water easily ran from the center to gutters on the shoulders constructed of paving bricks imbedded in cement. Drainage was important to prevent upheaval during frost cycles.

The walks were carefully constructed to widths between nine and thirty feet. One experimental section was covered with asphalt or what was then called Scharff pavement—a tar or pitch material, heated in a boiler and mixed with sand and gravel—which was poured on top of the walk bed and left to harden. In the late 1880s Prospect Park maintained its own asphalt plant and developed a formula that was the envy of engineers involved in Central Park. The walkways there were in a constant state of disintegration, and by 1888 asphalt hexagonal tiles, similar to those in place today, were introduced.

Vaux's Architectural Delights

Prospect Park's appeal came mostly from the artful treatment of the landscape, but the park also became a showcase for Vaux's architectural designs. Gone now are his original thatched, Adirondack-style shelters and the rustic bridges made of gnarled lengths of birch, locust, or oak that were erected throughout the

Silhouetted in afternoon sunlight, a biker rides along the Lake shoreline path originally designed as a promenade.

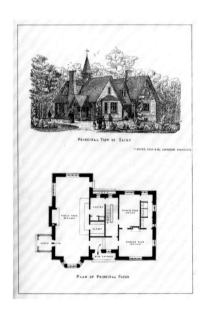

Located in the Ravine, the Dairy produced milk from the farm animals that grazed in the park.

grounds. Gone too are the two rustic shelters used by horsecar patrons that stood at Grand Army Plaza. The park's most prominent shelter, the Thatched Shelter, located about two hundred yards inside the plaza entrance, offered views of the Long Meadow. Across the lawn just off of East Drive stood a small shelter, and located in the Rose Garden was a heptagonal summerhouse, built of sassafras and cedar, that commanded views of the east woods and Battle Pass. At the magnificent Ambergill Shelter, cantilevered over the Ravine, visitors could sit in leafy seclusion and escape the day's heat while listening to the sound of water cascading over Ambergill Falls below.

The Lake's Promenade Drive Shelter offered "very agreeable views across the water, the north shore being the most picturesque."[14] This large, two-hundred-by-thirty-five-foot canopied structure was the centerpiece of the area and a main gathering point for visitors. Olmsted and Vaux wanted people to spend an entire day in the park and placed tables in some shelters where people could read or women could do needlepoint.

Vaux was a master at incorporating buildings and structures into the landscape. The Dairy, constructed of bluestone with Ohio sandstone, was a cozy farmhouse where visitors could buy milk and sandwiches, with a steeply pitched, gabled slate roof that was topped with a cupola. It was reminiscent of an English cottage and was tucked into the wooded crest of Sullivan Hill. The architect's Concert Grove was a combination of landscape and architectural design and, though less ornate and smaller in scale, was Prospect Park's equivalent of Central Park's Mall and Bethesda Terrace. Vaux planned the grove as a formal garden with angled walks bisecting a checkerboard of small lawns and raised flower beds in massive brownstone urns. Set against the slope of Breeze Hill, the Lake, and East Drive, the Concert Grove looked out to Music Island, separated from the shore by a slender channel of water. A stone balustrade with carved friezes and posts topped with flower urns surrounded much of the grove, and seating that overlooked East Drive allowed visitors to watch the ongoing procession of carriages.

The heavily planted urns that
originally stood atop ornate
pedestals at the Concert Grove's
hand-carved sandstone wall (seen
here in the 1890s) disappeared
in the 1940s. Reproductions were
installed as part of the Lakeside
restoration project.

This musical detail at the
Concert Grove was designed by
architect Thomas Wisedell, as were
the Concert Grove fountains.

TOP
Pictured here in 1910, the Concert Grove House (left) offered refreshments that could be enjoyed inside or at the adjacent Oriental Pavilion (right).

BOTTOM (LEFT AND RIGHT)
Intricacies in Vaux's architectural design are evident in the details at the Oriental Pavilion.

The Oriental Pavilion, an open-air shelter where visitors stopped for refreshment or to escape inclement weather, was directly in front of the Concert Grove House, which was designed in the popular Queen Anne style. The pavilion was imaginative in design and displayed Asian influences, which were prevalent in Vaux's work. It stood out, yet with its curvilinear and delicate lines, it was still unobtrusive.

The majority of the park's buildings were completed before 1873, as were most of the arches that offered previews to visitors and marked transitions between landscapes. The Nethermead Arches marked the end of the Ravine where it met the Nethermead, while the Endale and Meadowport Arches created entrances at the north end of the Long Meadow, and the Eastwood Arch provided an entrance near the Lullwater. The Cleft Ridge Span opened up a connection between the Concert Grove and the Lullwater.

The Meadowport Arch, with two entrances to the Long Meadow, was faced with Ohio sandstone; the Endale Arch, to the east of Meadowport Arch, was built with alternating blocks of Berea sandstone from Ohio and red-hued brownstone from New Jersey. The two colors of the latter structure display Syrio-Egyptian influence, while the Meadowport Arch resembles the Mogul architecture of India. The interior vaults of both arches were brick-lined with an overlay of tongue-and-groove black walnut and yellow pine in alternating strips to prevent moisture from dripping onto pedestrians. Benches, on which visitors could sit out storms, lined portions of the interior walls.

The interior of the Cleft Ridge Span was constructed of Béton Coignet concrete (patented in 1855), a mixture of limestone, cement, and sand, which was heated until it became a viscous paste and then poured into patterned molds to form intricate and multicolored ceiling designs. This added an artistic touch absent in the other arches. One of the new material's advantages was that it was considered practically impervious to water, and although lighter in weight than stone, it was said to be equal in strength, if not stronger. It was also used in the construction of the domed fountain in the Plaza and at St. Patrick's Cathedral in New York.

LEFT
The Endale Arch, seen here in the 1890s, was one of the first structures to be built in the park.

RIGHT
Passing through the Nethermead Arches, pictured in the 1890s, this path brings visitors out of the Ravine and into the open meadow. Of the three arches, one is for pedestrians, one for equestrians, and one for the Ambergill. Carriages would cross above.

OVERLEAF
A view through Meadowport Arch

RIGHT
Through the haze of a fall
afternoon, Meadowport Arch
looms like a Roman ruin.

BELOW
The Oriental Pavilion is framed
by the Cleft Ridge Span with its
Béton Coignet interior.

Unbuilt Structures

Several of Vaux's most elaborate designs were never built because of the Panic of 1873, which touched off a devastating international economic depression second only to the Great Depression. Brought on by unsuccessful railroad speculation and the collapse of banks, the panic lasted a decade, during which 25 percent of New York City's workforce was unemployed. The impact on Prospect Park was significant; only ongoing projects were completed, resulting in the cancellation of Vaux's Refectory, which was to be a major focal point. This restaurant was designed to be approached from the Concert Grove and Lookout Hill and had terraces cascading down to the Lake to provide additional access for boaters and skaters. Vaux's stone observation tower, resembling the bell tower in Venice's Piazza St. Marco, was also never erected. Planned for the top of Lookout Hill, it would have become the park's most visible landmark. The panic also eliminated additional archways at the park's south end and a shelter at the Carriage Concourse.

None of these cancellations lessened public enthusiasm for Prospect Park. Even before it was formally opened, visitors flocked to the site to see its construction. Old park antagonists softened, and some admitted that the money was well spent—the park was considered a gem. An *Eagle* reporter summed up the sentiment shared by most Brooklynites: The park was beginning to resemble nature "so very naturally that the old lady must begin to look after her laurels or she will soon be compelled to take lessons from art."[15]

Vaux's unbuilt design for the Carriage Concourse shelter featured a canopy approximately one hundred feet across to provide shade for carriages and horses.

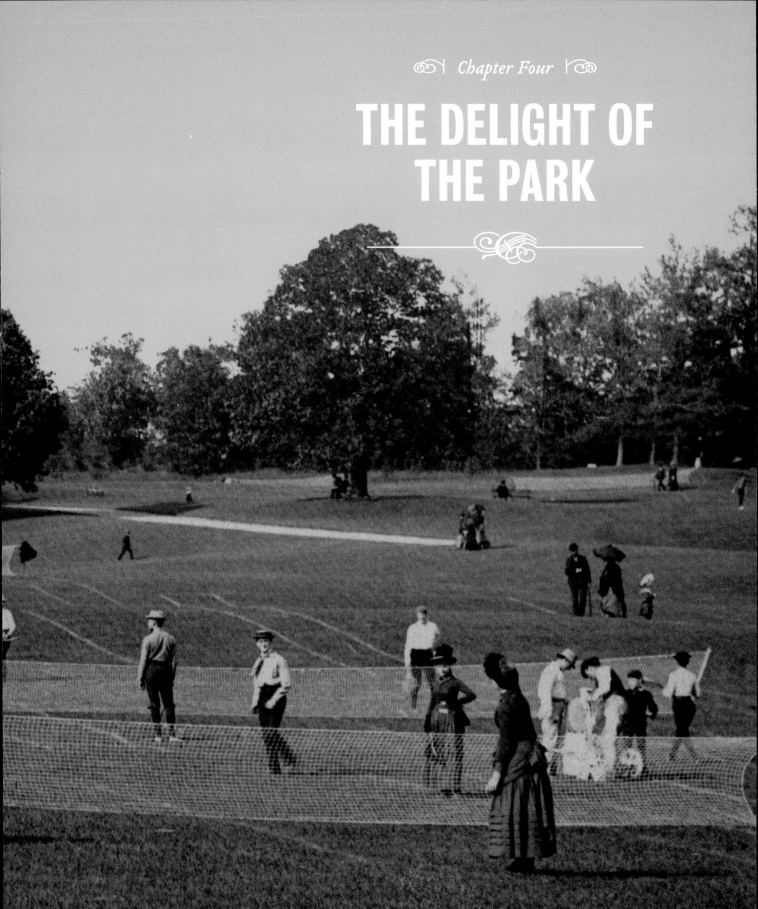

Chapter Four

THE DELIGHT OF THE PARK

Y 1872 JAMES STRANAHAN'S DREAM OF AN exquisite park for Brooklyn had been realized. "Tens of thousands of pent up denizens" visited Prospect Park soon after its opening to revel in the man-made and natural landscape.[1] Frederick Law Olmsted was thrilled by the public's enthusiastic reception. "In all my life I have never seen such joyous collections of people," he wrote. "I have, in fact, more than once observed tears of gratitude in the eyes of poor women, as they watched their children thus enjoying themselves."[2] He also felt satisfaction at seeing "invalids, aged people and convalescents…enjoying the air and the quiet which they found in the groves of the Park." Beginning in 1871 the Park Commission even provided wheelchairs for the disabled and elderly and later supplied baby carriages for parents for use in the park.

In the days before public understanding of viruses and bacteria, many believed that deadly diseases were contracted from the miasma that enveloped cities. Doctors often prescribed visits to parks rather than medication; the Massachusetts General Hospital even opened a suburban center, believing it would hasten patients' recovery with a change of air and scene.[3] Olmsted and Vaux, likewise, touted the park's health benefits. As Olmsted wrote, "Air is disinfected by sunlight and foliage…acts mechanically to purify the air by screening it."[4]

But visitors came mostly for the sheer pleasure of being in the park. People walked miles to "the one place where they can go without a cent in their pockets and still have a good time," the *Eagle* noted. Visitors strolled to the summit of Lookout Hill for the views and to the Concert Grove for band performances. They wandered through the woods and down to the Deer Paddock at the foot of Battle Pass. All around the park young men flirted with "white aproned" and comely nursemaids who tended to their "happy little occupants." A reporter noted in 1888 that there were hundreds of these "good looking nurse girls," and it was not long before the park became a romantic meeting place.[5]

The Long Meadow in those times did not have the flurry of physical activity that we see today but was instead a place of relaxation and peaceful strolling—ball playing and other strenuous activities were initially restricted to the Peninsula. A flock of white-faced sheep grazing in the meadow, with their lambs so tame that they ate from children's palms, added to the sense of tranquility. These New Hampshire and black-faced Southdown sheep were fixtures into the 1930s and served both aesthetic and practical purposes. As a design element they lent a fairy-tale air with their tending shepherds and dogs, while they kept the Long Meadow cropped and fertilized.

PREVIOUS
Lawn tennis on the Long
Meadow, 1885

Activities

Archery was one of the quiet amusements allowed on the Long Meadow. One can hardly imagine this activity being permitted anywhere in the park today because of safety concerns, but in 1881 the National Archery Association's annual tournament was held at the Parade Ground. *Harper's Weekly* noted that the field "dotted here and there with the party-colored targets, the gaily adorned tents, and the enclosure fringed with flags formed a beautiful setting for the archers, in costumes more or less picturesque, and the spectators, who treated the matter much as if it were a gigantic lawn party." The article went on to add that women liked archery because it was not strenuous and displayed their "pretty dresses and graceful attitudes as they sent flights of arrows on to the targets."[6]

Women, along with men, also took to croquet on the Long Meadow. Prospect Park croquet clubs were credited with preserving the game in the United States (one had to pay to play in Central Park or be a member of a club, but any player could join a match in Prospect Park). Brooklyn players pioneered new mallets and balls of different materials and rewrote the rules of the game. The croquet lawn, near the Third Street entrance, was in use even in winter when snow was swept away. The Croquet House was built in 1892 on the northwest perimeter of the Long Meadow to store equipment for the ever-growing number of players, including many aging Civil War veterans, who appeared regularly.

Lawn tennis became all the rage in the 1880s as enthusiasm for more active sports increased. The Park Commission eventually maintained three hundred courts on the Long Meadow and the Nethermead, which were rolled, watered, lined, and cut three times

It was common in these new urban parks to use sheep to maintain the meadows, as seen in this 1898 photo of Prospect Park.

In the late nineteenth century archery practice was a common sight in the park.

a week by teams of horses and with hand mowers until gas-powered mowers took over in the early part of the twentieth century. By then, Brooklyn was home to one-third of all the tennis courts in New York State.

What a surprise it would be today to emerge onto the Long Meadow to see scores of grass courts and hundreds of players dressed in a profusion of colors, "hurrying about in one confusing throng."[7] Edith Wharton wrote in *The Age of Innocence* (1920) that for women of the late nineteenth century, tennis was "too rough and inelegant for social occasions," but in reality they loved it.[8] Men wore long trousers or knickerbockers, while women wore loose white or blue flannel jackets with matching skirts—they also often held the racket in one hand and a parasol in the other. The only advantage to playing with a parasol, noted an *Eagle* reporter, is that it encouraged strengthening in both arms.[9] Tennis developed such a large following that in 1910 the Tennis House was erected on the edge of the Long Meadow to provide one thousand lockers for the players as well as storage space for nets and posts from the courts. Previous storage areas at the Music Pagoda and the Picnic Shelter, and in the basement of Litchfield Villa were already full.

Miniature-yacht racing was also a favorite pastime in the late nineteenth and early twentieth centuries. The six-foot boats came in greens, whites, reds, or natural mahogany varnished to a gleam. Sloops and schooners, like the *Cloud*, the *Zepher*, the *Mary Elizabeth*, and even the *John Y. Culyer*, shot across the Lake, heeling and dipping their masts, weaving in and out of spectator boats. Excitement mounted as the yachts rounded the marker buoy and headed for the finish line of the five-eighths-mile triangular course. "If you think the contestants are sailing their boats for nothing more than a little fun, you ought to watch their faces when the boats are nearing the finish," said the boathouse custodian. "One of our elderly members had to give up racing because his doctor told him the excitement was too much for his heart."[10] Miniature-yacht racing was held regularly until the 1930s.

The Lake was the center of activity year-round. Rowboating (boats rented for a dollar), canoeing, and fishing were popular, and pedal boats in the shape of large swans were available at the Upper Pool. Skating attracted huge crowds, sometimes as many as twenty thousand people. A red ball flag hoisted in Grand Army Plaza and red ball placards posted on the front of trolleys alerted visitors that the Lake and Lullwater ice was solid.

This early wooden boathouse (built in 1876) served as a shelter for skaters during winter.

Crowds of skaters on the Lullwater were often so thick that blue uniformed "keepers" dispersed them to prevent a breakthrough, while horse teams periodically planed and smoothed the ice. Elegant ladies might be cloaked in costly silk, velvets, and furs; most women wore flowing overcoats and ankle-length skirts. Men sported ulsters and bowlers, and occasionally a top hat. Skates could be rented, but "impecunious urchins" sometimes shared theirs, streaking off with one skate each.[11] Skating around the Lake while absorbing the beauty of the winter landscape was a celebratory event in Brooklyn. Even at night hundreds of swirling figures zipped along the Lullwater, lit by the soft amber light of lanterns. Their glow also reached across to the oak beams and stone blocks of the Lullwood Bridge. The nearby wooden boathouse, built across Binnen Falls and open in the summer, was enclosed for the winter, and four wood-burning stoves warmed numb feet and fingers while shivering skaters clutched mugs of hot coffee and cocoa they bought for a few cents.

Only a quarter of the Lake was available for skating, as other sections were reserved for curling, ice yachting, and ice-baseball games. The ten-player baseball teams (with two shortstops) skated around three-foot-square bases. In 1883 crowds gathered in the bitter cold to watch a Baltimore ice-baseball club defeat a hometown squad sixteen to fifteen.

Just as the Lake attracted crowds, so did the park's picnic areas, particularly at the Dairy, where the quiet, shady grounds drew visitors during summers. The cottage stood wonderfully secluded at the edge of the Midwood, just over the crest of Payne Hill (today's Sullivan Hill), where an ancient cut in the terminal moraine became a section of a bridle path that ran past the Dairy's rear entrance. Equestrians often rode up the cut and hitched their horses in a nearby shelter before snacking at the farmhouse. The surrounding woods were full of chipmunks, rabbits, and foxes, as well as robins, red-winged black-birds, finches, and cardinals. Trees included oaks, maples, ash, and pine, as well as some shrubs and plants many park users had never before seen, such as great-leaved magnolias, five-fingered akebias, and Sicilian sumacs. Olmsted and Vaux had imported new varieties of vegetation to enhance the beauty of the plantings.

As no drives extended to the Dairy, children could play there without fear of being run over by a carriage, and adults could relax and read or even doze. Chairs and tables were provided inside and outside on a grassy area where families could drink tea and coffee. Milk was also available warm or chilled, supplied by a half dozen Durham and Jersey cows that grazed on the Long Meadow and were stabled at a park farmstead just north of the Dairy. Fresh milk was a delicacy in the days before pasteurization and refrigeration, and offered a healthy alternative to the gray and watery swill milk produced by cows fed on the grain residue from Brooklyn's many distilleries.

The Dairy served ham, corned-beef, and tongue sandwiches, along with bread and cheese. There were platters of sardines, pickled oysters, biscuits, nuts, and sweets, such as ice cream, macaroons, and ladyfingers. Promoting the facility, Olmsted wrote:

> *A man from any class shall say to his wife, when he is going out in the morning, "My dear, when the children come home from school, put some bread and butter and salad in a basket and go to the chestnut tree where we found the Johnsons last week. I will join you there as soon as I can get away from the office. We will walk to the dairy-man's cottage and get some tea and some fresh milk for the children and take our supper by the brook-side."*[12]

Within a decade of the Dairy's opening, it became so crowded that the main picnic ground was moved across the Long Meadow to the larger lawn and shelter around the present-day Picnic House. Picnicking became a tradition so ingrained in Prospect Park that the *Eagle* proclaimed that it was more cherished than Fourth of July fireworks or Thanksgiving plum pudding and pumpkin pie.[13] By the 1920s the park provided 1,200 picnic tables, and even these were not enough to satisfy demand—people were asked to eat in shifts to accommodate availability of tables. Attire at these leisurely picnics was extraordinarily formal by today's standards. One Brooklyn resident remembered his grandmother at a summer picnic dressed in a full-length black-taffeta gown, black-velvet choker, and frilly garden hat decked with heirloom papier-mâché roses.[14]

Visitors to the park included many New Yorkers from across the river. Brooklynites were vexed that these New York interlopers disrupted the park's calm and dignity, appearing in inappropriate dress, "hatless and coatless men and dirty women, before whom was spread the remains of a lunch not too inviting, to say the least."[15] Local residents also complained that Manhattan's poor came to steal the park's flowering shrubs and leave their food wrappings behind. The *Eagle* reported on the plight of New Yorkers, whose Central Park prohibited picnics: "The park authorities of Gotham would shudder at the thought of picnic parties in Central Park, where the grass is sacred to sheep but denied to children."[16] By contrast, it was not a crime in Prospect Park

for a visitor to "lie supine upon the grass and devour his lunch in the Roman style, using the splendid turf for a triclinium."[17]

Not all was supine in the park, however. Maypole dancing and the annual Sunday School Parade were community celebrations that continued well into the twentieth century. Young girls wearing white middy blouses, skirts, kerchiefs, and yellow, red, and blue berets performed folk dances and wove bright streamers in intricate patterns. The Sunday School Parade, sponsored by the Brooklyn Sunday School Union, dated back to 1830. Public-school children were given a day off during the school week to march through the borough in various parades. Some ended at the Long Meadow, where participants passed before city dignitaries, former U.S. presidents, and as many as fifteen thousand spectators seated in temporary stands.

Children especially loved the goat carriages and pony rides available in the park. In the 1890s Thomas F. "Santa Claus" Rochford offered five-cent goat rides in the park, which began at the Willink entrance. Goats were ubiquitous in Brooklyn and could be found, as Rochford said, on every hill near the park and along Eastern Parkway, and purchased for $2.21. The goat carriages were expensive woodworking creations that could carry up to six delighted children. Pony or donkey rides were held near the Menagerie, where children could ride three times around a circuit for a dime. The children often complained that the horses trotted so fast that the fun was over before it began. They preferred the donkey "of preternatural sageness and steadiness," who went at a much slower pace.[18]

The First Carousel

Attracted by parallel bars, swings, and seesaws, along with a croquet lawn and a maze, families congregated in the Rose Garden and Vale of Cashmere—which was by then known as the Children's Playground. The adults escaped the heat of a summer day in a nearby shelter, while the children romped among the shrubs or sailed boats in the pond. The greatest attraction in the Rose Garden was the Carousel, erected in 1874 and propelled by "an old, white and blind horse" that had toiled round and round for years in the darkness of the cellar."[19] Smaller than the present one near the Willink entrance and featuring only twenty-four wooden horses and four coaches, the Carousel whirled as the organ blared and children soared for only three cents a ride. The lack of shade and the heat in the Vale of Cashmere eventually forced closure of the playground around 1890, and the upper portion was transformed into the Rose Garden. But the Carousel was so popular that the park board recommended that a second one be built near the picnic grounds.

The vale is one of the more exquisite spots in Prospect Park. Situated in a depression that had once been a kettle pond, it is a miniature Shangri-la, isolated from the rest of the park by plantings and geography (a section of the terminal moraine separates it from Flatbush Avenue and enhances its bucolic isolation). Despite its beauty and allure, it was so well hidden that few Brooklynites were aware of its existence even thirty years after the park opened.

Maypole dancing on the north end of the Long Meadow, c. 1900.

In the 1890s children could take a ride in a goat-pulled carriage, pictured here in front of the Cleft Ridge Span.

The Children's Playground as seen in the 1890s. It was radically redesigned by McKim, Mead & White and is now called the Vale of Cashmere.

Carriage Rides

A long-forgotten pleasure in Prospect Park was the evening carriage ride on the drives. At the end of the day, wealthy couples—the children left at home with their nannies—would circle the park in carriages, taking in snippets of beauty through the trees. The promenade of carriages along the drives continued after sunset, illuminated by gas streetlights and the warm glow of carriage lamps. (In hopes of a tip, boys with matches in hand often scurried up to the coachmen to light the lamps.) Many took in the view of the Atlantic from the top of Breeze Hill, while others stopped at Nellie's Lawn, named in memory of a young woman who had come regularly to this small, peaceful meadow with her mother. The two had spent much time sitting and reading under a large elm that grew near the East Drive. When Nellie embarked on a European tour and died of "the fever" in Rome, the park, at her mother's request, placed a plaque on the tree, inscribed "Nellie's Tree," and the nearby meadow eventually took her name.[20]

The carriages were colorful sights to park visitors. Barouches and other popular carriages of the day were drawn by pairs, four-in-hands, and tandems of glistening horses, highly polished harnesses shining in the sun. The coachman, in a varnished topper, sat erect on his seat with whip at attention on the hip. Behind him on softly upholstered cushions of Bedford cord lolled the lady of the house, parasol properly cocked. The master was beside her, carnation in lapel, fragrant cigar jutting from beneath his walrus mustache.[21]

Carriage riding became so popular that a "coaching carnival" was held in 1891, during which thirty thousand waving, cheering spectators lined the Promenade, East Drive, and Ocean Parkway. "Ponderous coaches with four tiers of gaily-attired men and women, dainty carts, drawn tandems and tiny rigs with ponies between the shafts and small children at the ribbons," as well as some two hundred equestrians, passed by for hours and hours.[22]

During those years the drives were places where "opulence and fashion could air themselves…a place to see and be seen." In the winter, sleighs replaced the carriages. The drives were largely where the well-to-do enjoyed the park's loveliness, as did Brooklyn's minister and abolitionist Henry Ward Beecher, who contemplated his fate while riding in his carriage through Prospect Park during his infamous adultery trial.[23] Rides became available to the masses in the 1870s, when public carriages—beginning at the Plaza and Willink entrances—offered tours of the park.

Military Parades and Sports Events

With the carriage procession attracting great crowds, the military-drill and military-dress parades at the Parade Ground were guaranteed to draw many curious bystanders as well. Thousands came through the northeast entrance, which was flanked by two Revolutionary War cannons—one captured from the British at the Battle of Saratoga, the other taken at the Battle of Princeton. In May 1881 the members of the National Guard of New York's Twenty-second and Twenty-third Regiments marched in their summer-white duck pantaloons, blue tunics, and "belts pipeclayed to dazzling brightness and brasses burnished until they shone again." With the Grenadier band leading, the soldiers moved smartly across the drill field, "their white horsehair plumes waving in the wind." This parade, wrote an *Eagle* reporter, was "the handsomest ceremony seen on the parade ground in many a year….The sound off was as charming a military picture as could well be imagined, the regiment standing immovably at parade rest….As if in sympathy with the beauty of the scene, the sun left off sulking, brightening up by degrees…and at last bursting forth in full glory."[24] Similar parades continued into the twentieth century, when the Navy obtained permission for the sailors of the superdreadnought *Wyoming* to drill on the Parade Ground in 1914.

The general use of the Parade Ground changed soon after the park opened, however, as it increasingly became an arena for baseball, football, rugby, cricket, and lacrosse matches, as well as the occasional polo match, and later even for lawn bowling. Manhattan sporting clubs, lacking a similar facility in New York City, also began using the ground.

The first baseball game played on the Parade Ground was in 1873, when the Flatbush Eagles took to the field; henceforth the grounds were filled with the "nines" of baseball associations from across New York, including the Bedfords, the Commercials, and the Franklins. One of many leagues, the Brooklyn Amateur Association fielded the Vernons, the Ivanhoes, the Resolutes, the Oxfords, the Lafayettes, and the Atlas clubs. In 1884 play on all but one of the fields halted as fifteen thousand spectators watched the championship game between the Dauntlesses and the Stars, both of the Long Island Association. The former won. By 1886 as many as fifty baseball matches were held every day.

Cricket competed with baseball at the Parade Ground in terms of space, spectators, and participants. The sport had been played in America since the mid-1700s, and the Parade Ground offered an athletic ground that attracted teams from all over. In the fall of 1885, the Manhattan Cricket Club even played a team composed of D'Oyly Carte Opera Company cast members touring the United States with a production of *The Mikado*. The club also took on the St. Paul's School cricket team from New Hampshire—which they soundly defeated. Newspapers reported on cricket matches using distinctly British terms: the bowling was "on the spot," and St. Paul's made "a plucky stand."[25]

Polo, another popular import from England, drew ten thousand fans for a match between the Westchester Polo Club and Queens County Hunt in 1878. The sport grew, and the Polo Association's championship tournament—the equivalent to today's U.S. Open Polo Championships—was held at the Parade Ground in 1896. Four clubs of "men of leisure galloped about under the admiring eyes of an estimated 20,000 spectators, many of them 'members of the hunting set.'"[26] Mrs. Jack Gardner, a leading nineteenth-century arts patron who was always faithful to her Boston home team, the Myopias, brought a special party to Brooklyn for the tournament where New York's William Waldorf Astor presented the gold cup.[27]

During the late nineteenth century, the Parade Ground was closed for athletic events on Sundays, but in 1912 restrictions were lifted, precipitating a row with the clergy. The Reverend Dr. Edwin Dunton Bailey, pastor of the Prospect Heights Presbyterian Church, demanded that the law be rescinded and warned, "If you turn loose a Sabbath-breaking crowd in Prospect Park, near which church and homes are located, you make the task of training good citizens more difficult and you imperil the wholesome life we are trying to live."[28] The mayor compromised and restricted Sunday play to the afternoons, but many righteous churchgoers were not appeased.

Bicycling

If bicycling is ubiquitous in Prospect Park today, it was equally popular in the years after the park first opened. There were velocipedes with two small front wheels and a big back wheel, as well as those with one big front wheel and two small back wheels, bicycles, tricycles, quadricycles, and tandems. In 1884 the Park Commission first proposed a mile-long velocipede course for "wheelmen," but complaints mounted about bicycles spooking horses—for example, a young rider was killed near the park when she fell from a runaway horse startled by a bicyclist.[29] The commission at this time restricted bikes to the walkways but the public soon warmed to them, and the *New York Times* opined, "It is common experience the world over that a horse cares nothing about a bicycle the second time he sees it."[30]

In 1885 the League of American Wheelmen organized a parade of bikers to persuade the park administration to open the drives. Bikers dressed in broadcloth suits of greens, blues, and browns came

The park was a favorite spot for bicycling clubs. Photo, c. 1890s.

out to influence the "hard-hearted Park Commissioners…not touched by the poetry of the wheel."[31] The following year, Park Superintendent John Y. Culyer suspended restrictions limiting bicycles to the paths, as long as the wheelmen followed prescribed rules: no speeding, bugles, or whistles were allowed on the drives, and the riders had to have lighted lamps after sundown.[32]

In 1891 crowds lined the streets around Prospect Park when more than one thousand "knights and ladies of the wheel" rode down Flatbush Avenue in a bike parade, passing by Brooklyn Mayor Alfred Chapin and other dignitaries attending the show.[33] At one time it was said that no respectable woman would ride a bike, but the ladies division drew the most attention, their bikes bedecked with ribbons and flowers: "One woman rode a wheel entirely of gilt, and wore a gold dress, draped with black lace. Another had a great floral umbrella over her head." One participant rode with a "kid-karrier," a small seat between the saddle and the handle, which held "a sweet-faced little baby girl."[34]

Then as now, track squads used the park for training. The Harriers were a well-known local squad participating in an 1889 cross-country race that began at Washington Park, passed through Prospect Park, and ended back at Washington Park. Runners also ran moonlight races, "making the occasional wayfarer wonder whether he had seen ghosts or flitting figures in real flesh."[35] In 1906 Prospect Park hosted the first cross-country championship meet for the high-school boys of Greater New York, on a course that wound through the park and ended at the Parade Ground. In 1919 the park was the site for the national high-school track championships.

Music in the Park

From its beginnings Prospect Park hosted band concerts of all types, and in the 1870s performances were scheduled every Saturday afternoon from early June to late September. Among the popular groups of that period was the Twenty-Third Regiment Band, conducted by Luciano Conterno, which played both classical and popular music, including "The Grand March" from Richard Wagner's *Tannhäuser*, selections from Giuseppe Verdi's *La Traviata*, E. C. Phelps's the "Grand March 'Stranahan,'" and "Scotch Melodies," arranged by Conterno himself.

Music Island, a part of the Concert Grove, was the stage for these concerts, and the audience gathered around it. Some remained in the Concert Grove House, listening as they dined, or relaxed under the Oriental Pavilion. Others were in rowboats on the Lake, in their carriages on the Concourse, or on Breeze Hill. One of Olmsted and Vaux's major concepts in the park's original design was the use of this southeast quadrant by the Lake as the park's center of gravity—it incorporated Lookout Hill, the Promenade, the Promenade Drive Shelter, Breeze Hill, and the Concert Grove, with Music Island as the magnet.

The acoustics around Music Island, however, were poor, and during concerts "the breeze which wafted the strains over the water of the Lake…played sad havoc with the harmony. Discontented listeners

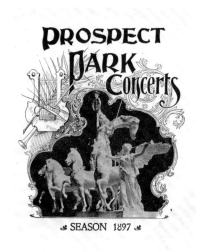

A program for a park concert in 1897

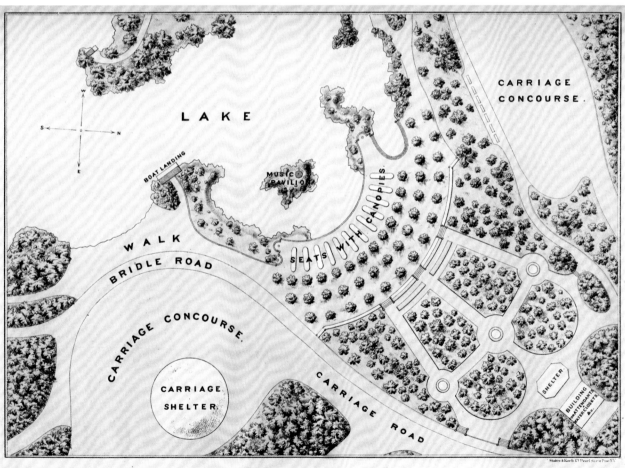

DESIGN FOR THE ARRANGEMENT OF PEDESTRIAN CONCOURSE.

SCALE: 120 FEET TO ONE INCH.

left their seats and strolled nearer the water's edge as the struggling melodies were dissipated by wind before they reached the banks or were drowned out by the shouts of exuberant children at play."[36]

In the early 1880s, in response to these problems, the park commissioners shifted concerts to a temporary music shelter by the Lullwater. Then in 1887, concerts moved to the Music Pagoda, newly built in a stand of London plane trees adjacent to the Nethermead. The pagoda's ceiling was specifically constructed to act as a sounding board to project music into the Nethermead, where as many as twenty-five thousand people could gather. By then Olmsted was no longer affiliated with Prospect Park except as an occasional consultant, but he complained that no effort was made to preserve Music Island as a venue by improving the acoustics with what he believed were simple measures. In a letter to Vaux, he wrote that Music Island was the soul of the Concert Grove and to abandon it was "simply absurd. It is a play of *Hamlet* with Hamlet omitted. Yet nobody in Brooklyn seems to have recognized it and I am driven to ask, 'Am I crazy or is it the others who are so?'"[37]

The Flower Craze

In the 1890s both Music Island and Lookout Hill became sites of large gardens as a flower craze swept through Prospect Park. In fact, Music Island was planted with such a profusion of red flowers that it became known as Scarlet Island. Olmsted once mused about parks "gay with flowers" and cautioned that too many would detract from the overall plan. He told Stranahan: "You know my opinion of the ridiculous little pies of bedding plants. Except for some few on the

Concert Grove, they are as much out of place as mosaic broaches on a Guernsey shirt."[38] But he could not stop the momentum. The stone stairway that led from the Concert Grove to the summit of Breeze Hill, was flanked by flower beds. The Camera Obscura was removed from Breeze Hill in 1890 and was replaced with a unique, umbrella-shaped shelter and an old-fashioned garden filled with poppies, hollyhocks, brown corn, morning glories, and many other varieties. Gardens were also planted at the temporary music shelter, at the Dairy, and in the vale by Litchfield Villa. An *Eagle* reporter noted that the park appeared as though touched by a fairy wand: "Hundreds of the sweetest scented flowers…bloom in profusion, and curious and dainty leaved plants from all countries of the earth charm the eye of the weary city visitor."[39] In one fall season alone, 125,000 flower bulbs were planted for spring flowering. At another time, 3,000 rose bushes were spread throughout the park. The Rose Garden became known as a flower mecca where "the rarest of roses and lilies bloom."[40] In 1897 a great event occurred for flower lovers: the blossoming of the Victoria Regia, "the queen among the lilies and the giantess among water flowers."[41] The park's gardeners, having tried unsuccessfully for years to raise a Victoria Regia, finally succeeded. This was the first blooming of the flower in the United States.

The flower craze had origins as early as 1875, when Beecher suggested that a greenhouse be built near Litchfield Villa. Not long thereafter the new facility opened and hosted flower shows that became regular attractions from the late nineteenth century through the first half of the twentieth century. In 1889 the park department centralized its nurseries in Prospect Park and built new propagating houses while renovating older greenhouses. Visitors came by the thousands to see the greenhouse displays of flowering bulbs, chrysanthemums, tropical plants, and cacti. In 1900 the large Palm House was built, followed by the Cactus House. Several propagation houses were also built near the Willink entrance. By the 1930s there were eighteen greenhouses and propagation houses in the park, mostly just south of Litchfield Villa at Prospect Park West and Seventh Street, on ground that is today used for a parks department garage and maintenance center.

Greenhouses were not the only new structures at Prospect Park. Although most work had ceased after the Panic of 1873, a flurry of new construction began following the economic recovery in the 1880s. The Picnic Shelter on the site of the present-day Picnic House was built, and a zoo was erected near the summit of Sullivan Hill, north of the Dairy. It housed elephants, lions, birds, monkeys, and bears, including the "diabolical" cinnamon bear "Spite," who, in 1902, had been transferred from the New York Zoological Park.[42]

Maintenance, Maintenance, Maintenance

The joy visitors of Prospect Park experienced—in its beauty, sports, picnics, and other offerings—obscured the difficult task of keeping the park operational. Though it was successfully accommodating growth and changes in activities, preserving the integrity of the designers' intent with the original plan was a challenge. Stranahan foresaw this in 1871 when he declared, "I built the park…the work of maintaining it will be done by another set of men."[43] Few then recognized the significance of his words.

Throughout the park's history, hurricanes, blizzards, electrical storms, tornadoes, draughts, and flooding wreaked havoc on it—as did the effects of air pollution, tussock moths, tent caterpillars, Dutch elm disease, and chestnut blight (which killed 1,400 trees). In February 1892, a severe ice storm damaged hundreds of trees in the woodlands, requiring 3,700 truckloads to remove the debris. It took many years for the forest to recover.

Mother Nature wasn't the only force that battered the park. People did the most damage, loving the park nearly to death. The wear and tear began as soon as it opened, with fifty-four thousand people visiting Prospect Park in 1868 when it was still barely half complete. A year later there were 2.1 million visitors, and in 1873, 6.7 million. By 1900, 15 million people were coming annually. In 1871, despite the presence of "park keepers" to protect the plantings, "all of the herbage and…the foliage growing within six feet of the ground, except a few briery thickets, wholly disappeared, the soil was worn to dust and blown and washed away so that within two years the roots of trees protruded and many withered in consequence. Whenever it rained, the old woods trails gullied. The hollow places became sloughs and the whole surface slimy and disagreeable to see or to walk on."[44]

Foot traffic between the Picnic Shelter and the Dairy was so heavy and the wear on the Long Meadow so extensive that the Park Commission proposed building a new walk to connect the two.

In the early twentieth century, the park featured several areas with flower beds, but they eventually proved too hard to maintain.

Flowering magnolia trees delight visitors in today's park.

Its concerns were reflected in the annual report of 1887: "The grass has been worn away, and the ground has become hard enough to turn water. Until this season the soil has had constant use for fifteen years, having had no rest or nourishment and but little moisture.… To allow this to continue would result in killing the trees and disfiguring the Park."[45]

In 1892 the administration noted that "much work remains to be done to bring Prospect Park up to what it should be," adding that "the slopes and ravines surrounding the Farm House, the sides of Lookout Hill and the section around the deer pond are in imperative need of resoiling. Much of the rock work along the line of the brook needs repairing and rebuilding."[46] The dilapidated walks also needed to be resurfaced with asphalt. Earlier, in 1888, Chapin found Prospect Park rundown, with unsafe bridges and the wooden picket fence around the park falling down.[47] Chapin recommended spending $100,000 to make the necessary repairs.

The meadows, the woodlands, and the Lake were neglected, as were the streams, which each became choked, sitting stagnant in pools. The Lake in fact became so stagnant during the late 1880s that the park commissioners considered turning it into a large meadow. The rustic wooden bridges and shelters rotted, and the arbors and benches had to be rebuilt with more durable locust wood. Sledding children destroyed and damaged shrubs as they raced down hillsides onto the Nethermead or the Long Meadow, and the sled runners gouged the dormant grass. Skaters clipped branches and destroyed shrubs along the lakeshore. Vandals stripped and girdled trees and stole shrubbery even when it was surrounded by barbed wire. The administration lamented the damage, which extended even to the flower garden in front of Litchfield Villa. It wasn't just the foot pounding—people also left behind piles of garbage and food. "Big slices of watermelon, lemon, orange skins, muskmelons, meat and cheese sandwiches" were all discarded after one particularly bad weekend.[48]

Olmsted had stressed that to ensure quality maintenance and preservation it was more important for a park to have continuity of management than for most other organizations. For nearly twenty years during the early days of Prospect Park, it was fortunate to have Culyer serve as chief engineer. He was employed from the beginning of construction as part of the Olmsted-Vaux team and had already worked under the partners during the construction of Central Park in the late 1850s. During the Civil War he served in the Union army and was later an assistant to Olmsted on the Sanitary Commission. When both Olmsted and Vaux resigned from Prospect Park in 1873, Culyer became the superintendent; and after Stranahan left the Park Commission in 1882, he remained to preserve the designers' original vision.

Culyer constantly labored with inadequate funds for repairs and restoration. Struggling to juggle the park's needs with the available financial resources, he became the target of much public criticism, even anonymous death threats—policemen had to be stationed outside of his house. Yet Culyer persisted, saying that "the severity of the criticism is seldom tempered with any consideration of the circumstances under which the work was performed." He understood the park's importance to the citizens of Brooklyn and claimed that "the money expended on them is an investment whose dividends are returned to the visitors in a thousand channels."[49] Culyer lamented the political-spoils system that contributed to the park's deterioration. He tried to hire only skilled personnel with no connection to the political bosses who were accustomed to rewarding cronies and buying votes with jobs, but his efforts were not always successful, and the workers who maintained the park were often untrained.

It was not just the machine politics that deprived the park of proper support over the years, however. When reform administrations reduced taxes, Prospect Park took immediate cuts. In almost every recession, from 1873 to 2008, park budgets were among the first to be attacked, as political leaders tend to get little admonition for slashing maintenance funds.

Monuments and buildings, on the other hand, are amortized over decades and can be financed even in lean years—politicians can point to them as evidence of their good deeds. Even though the park has been in dire need of maintenance funding throughout most of its existence, major capital projects were undertaken over the years, including new buildings that altered the architectural character of the park. In light of these hurdles, Olmsted and Vaux's initial design concepts were often neglected as the park evolved.

New Architectural Styles and Major Capital Projects

By the 1890s the City Beautiful movement, whose proponents believed that a beautiful city would inspire its inhabitants to moral and civic virtue, greatly influenced the development of Prospect Park and created a new layer of architectural design in its landscape. Filled with the wealth and optimism that came with the economic recovery from the wrenching 1873 depression and the belief that they were heirs to Western civilization, Americans embraced the beauty and elegance of European classical architecture: cities with wide boulevards and stately beaux-arts public buildings. This was mirrored in the elaborate neoclassical buildings of the still-celebrated 1893 World's Columbian Exposition in Chicago, which marked the four hundredth anniversary of Columbus's discovery of America and is often regarded as the showpiece for the movement. The exposition grounds and landscaping were designed by Olmsted.

Even before the Columbian Exposition opened, the park was already replacing some of its more rustic structures. Both the Terrace Bridge, designed by Vaux in 1890, and the McKim, Mead & White Lullwater Bridge (1890) replaced preexisting simpler designs. The iron span of the new Terrace Bridge was imposing, although somewhat outsized, and was supported by handsome arched-steel trusses resting on stately brownstone abutments. The cast-iron Lullwater Bridge, which frames today's Boathouse and the upper

OVERLEAF
The iron-clad Terrace
Bridge between the Lullwater
and the Lake

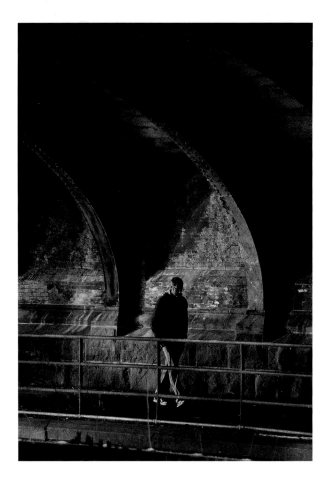

part of the Lullwater, was graceful and more delicate. The bridge's ornamental design extended to its underside for the pleasure of boaters and skaters that passed beneath.

The City Beautiful movement also brought a new look to the Plaza. The original Olmsted and Vaux design was simple and naturalistic and created a public gathering space that was also the major entryway to the park. The redesign of the Plaza transformed it into the second most important symbol of Brooklyn's growth after the Brooklyn Bridge, built in 1883. Paved with Belgian blocks, the original Plaza was bereft of significant embellishment or structures, with only an isolated statue of President Abraham Lincoln standing behind a fountain. For much of its early history the Plaza was regarded as an expanse to be avoided: "No one cares to cross it. It is devoid of all life and is a stony waste," the park directors declared.[50] And it remained so until the 1890s, when it was redesigned as a space big enough to accommodate large crowds. The new square assumed considerable significance for Prospect Park, largely because Central Park lacked an equal entrance.

The Plaza's redesign extended to its fountain. The original simple water-jet fountain had been replaced in 1873 with a Vaux-designed, double-domed version of cast iron and Béton Coignet that had horizontal and vertical water jets as well as twenty-four colored-glass windows lit by gas lamps. In 1897 Vaux's fountain was superseded by an electric one with a prismatic water display, designed by T. W. Darlington, that was similar to, but larger than, the famous World's

Columbian Exposition fountain from four years prior. A series of lamps, parabolic mirrors, and colored glass, blended with two thousand jets, ball sprays, straight sprays, ring fans, and funnels were made a "mesmerizing kaleidoscope of colors" by an operator seated below.[51] The *Eagle* called the new fountain the finest and largest in the world, and on its first night twenty thousand visitors witnessed a magnificent water and light show. It became the Plaza's star attraction, and crowds repeatedly came to watch the display. The electric fountain remained until 1932, when it was demolished to accommodate subway construction, and the existing Bailey Fountain was installed. (The new fountain was designed by Edgerton Swarthout and features the allegorical and mythical figures of Neptune and male and female nudes that represent wisdom and felicity. Eugene Francis Savage sculpted the figures.)

The focal point of the Plaza became a majestic memorial arch, later named the Soldiers and Sailors Memorial, drafted by John H. Duncan, designer of Grant's Tomb in Riverside Park, which honors Union Civil War veterans. The construction of the arch took place between 1889 and 1892. It was dedicated by General William Tecumseh Sherman, with President Grover Cleveland laying the cornerstone. Although smaller, the eighty-by-eighty-foot arch resembles the classical style of the Arc de Triomphe. When first completed, the memorial was still bare of adornment, but in 1895 artists Thomas Eakins (known mainly for his paintings) and William R. O'Donovan were commissioned to create the bronze relief panels depicting Lincoln and General Ulysses S. Grant astride their horses. The panels, originally meant to cover the front of the arch, were criticized for their odd proportions and for their lack of grandeur and were moved to the inner faces of the arch piers. At the suggestion of McKim, Mead & White two new bronze figure groups by sculptor Frederick MacMonnies were placed on the front. One depicts a trumpeting Valkyrie summoning Union army soldiers into the chaos and horror of battle—officers with flashing bayonets and rifles, a fallen horse, a wounded drummer, and a young officer (resembling MacMonnies) with his sword held high complete the scene. (The group is remarkably similar to François Rude's work on the Arc de Triomphe.) The other, more static sculpture depicts Navy sailors on the deck of a disabled ship preparing to engage the enemy. An interesting detail is the African American sailor, pistol in hand, in the foreground. (Images of African Americans were rare at that time.) MacMonnies's arresting bronze figure of Columbia, the mythical personification of America, and her quadriga, a four-horse-drawn chariot, were placed atop the arch.

A pair of Doric shafts designed by Duncan and capped by MacMonnies's bronze eagles was erected on either side of the park's main entrance. McKim, Mead & White added two identical columns—one on the Flatbush Avenue side of the entrance and the other by Prospect Park West. These created symmetry and were complemented by curving balustrades that abutted pedestals supporting bronze urns. Just behind the balustrades and flanking the entrance, two twelve-sided Italianate pavilions with Guastavino

New technology allowed elaborate displays of colored light and water at the fountain in the Plaza, as shown in the park's annual report of 1897.

LEFT
The Soldiers and Sailors Memorial
Arch was dedicated in 1892.

RIGHT
Neptune and his accompanying
figures grace the most recent
of four fountains that have stood
on the Plaza at the park's main
entrance.

ceiling tiles were constructed to replace two Vaux-designed horse-car stops. Guastavino tiles are found in many of New York's graceful buildings, such as the Cathedral of Saint John the Divine, the Great Hall at Ellis Island, and the Grand Central Oyster Bar, and are also used in the park's other beaux-arts structures, such as the Boathouse, the Tennis House, the Peristyle, and the Willink Comfort Station. The new splendor at the Plaza also included the removal of the picket fence that once surrounded the park and the addition of stone walls and iron fencing.

The main entrance was not the only one that was redesigned. McKim, Mead & White replaced all of the park's entryways with grandiose schemes that were the antithesis of Olmsted and Vaux's organic simplicity. Charles McKim, who studied at the Ecole des Beaux-Arts in Paris and whose style was emblematic of the beaux-arts approach, was a leader in the planning of the World's Columbian Exposition, just as Olmsted was in its landscape design. McKim made Brooklyn a showcase for the work of his firm, designing not only the park entrances and the Peristyle (1903) at the park's southern end but also the nearby Brooklyn Botanic Garden administration building and the Brooklyn Museum.

The new Parkside Avenue entrance by McKim, Mead & White, at the junction of Parkside and Ocean Avenues, featured a pergola made of a granite colonnade with stone screens and lined with benches. Covered in wisteria, the pergola's splash of color still draws visitors into the park. The Park Circle entryway displays

MacMonnies's *Horse Tamers*—massive, life-sized bronze horses carrying nude male riders and rearing up on nineteen-foot granite pedestals on each side of the roadway. The Bartel-Pritchard entrance columns at Fifteenth Street and Prospect Park West are loose replicas of the Acanthus Column at Delphi in Greece. The Third Street entrance was embellished in 1897 with a pair of bronze pumas sculpted by Alexander Phimister Proctor and set on imposing rectangular granite foundations. All entrances, except for the one at Third Street, were recessed into the park, the Willink entrance at Flatbush Avenue being the most pronounced.

Olmsted complained that the changes to the park were destroying his original design. He could write philosophically about parks, stating once: "After we have left them, they have been more or less barbarously treated, yet they stand. They are 100 years ahead of any spontaneous public demand…and they have a manifestively civilizing effect."[52] But that didn't limit his concerns. He specifically objected to the makeover of the Children's Playground made by McKim, Mead & White, which incorporated new walkways, balustrades, and three basins—two of these displayed flowering aquatic plants, and a third featured a fountain by MacMonnies. Olmsted also disliked the area's name change from Children's Playground to Vale of Cashmere, because it didn't conform to his unembellished ideals. In a letter to Park Commissioner Frank Squier, Olmsted wrote, "I feel it my duty to record my professional opinion against changing the space intended to be devoted to a children's playground into a rose garden.…I am told…that you are further intending to introduce considerable architectural constructions into the dell which has been absurdly named the Vale of Cashmere. I beg leave to ask you to pause before making such a questionable departure from the established design of the park."[53] According to Olmsted, the new administration offered little devotion to the original plan and had little understanding of Olmsted and Vaux's concept of landscape design.

Olmsted voiced other complaints as well: "We can hardly avoid a feeling that there is an unfortunate tendency to crowd Prospect Park too much with statues, monuments, and other architectural structures," he again wrote to Squier in a letter dated 1895, the year of his

retirement. "If this tendency continues, and more and more architectural features are introduced, the time will come when the beautiful, quiet, rural landscapes of the Park will be, to a very great extent, marred, and the Park made to resemble a confused and fussy-looking ornamental garden, or the best of our rural cemeteries."[54] Efforts to decorate the park with monuments and statues had begun as early as July 1871, when, following European trends, the city unveiled a large bust of the writer Washington Irving near the Concert Grove. It was donated by Demas Barnes, a prominent businessman and former congressman, who believed that the "empty" landscape needed adornment. In the same year, Beecher compared Prospect Park to an ancient Greek temple, with statues of the noblest citizens cast in marble, ivory, and gold. "I doubt not that in such a city as Brooklyn there will yet be found scores who will seek the honor of placing statues in this Park."[55] In 1873 a massive bronze bust of poet and playwright John Howard Payne, who gained fame as lyricist for the wildly popular song "Home Sweet Home," was dedicated as spectators filling the meadow around Sullivan Hill were serenaded by the Twenty-Third Regiment Band. Composers' busts were placed in the Concert Grove; some, like the one of Ludwig van Beethoven, were contributed by the German Singers of Brooklyn, who had won them in national competitions in Philadelphia and New York; others, by various groups celebrating their cultural and national heritage.

Emphasizing his resistance to this adornment, Olmsted wrote, "The Park is a work of art, designed to produce certain affects upon the minds of men. There should be nothing in it, absolutely nothing—not a foot of surface nor a spear of grass—which does not represent, study, design a sagacious consideration & application… to that end."[56] To this day the interior of the park remains free of statuary, but the Concert Grove, the Plaza, and the park's other entrances are veritable open-air sculpture museums that include a vast collection of MacMonnies's pieces, ranging from his impressive Columbia and quadriga to his stunning *Horse Tamers*.

MacMonnies had risen to prominence for his elaborate fountain of Columbia in her Grand Barge of State at the World's Columbian Exposition in Chicago. In New York he is perhaps best known for his figure of Nathan Hale, arms pinioned, feet bound, erected in front of City Hall in 1893. A Brooklyn Heights native raised by his American mother and Scottish-born father, he began modeling figures at the age of five. He first sculpted with his own chewing gum, then moved on to dough found in his mother's kitchen before he discovered clay.

At the age of seventeen MacMonnies was a studio assistant to the noted sculptor Augustus Saint-Gaudens before he studied at the Ecole des Beaux-Arts. Most of MacMonnies's work at Prospect Park is located around the Plaza. In addition to Columbia, the arch's bas-reliefs, and the eagles atop the entrance columns, he created the equestrian statue of Civil War General Henry Warner Slocum with his sword raised high. Just inside the entrance of the park is his statue of Stranahan. The artist was meticulous in his craftsmanship and had Stranahan's hands cast in plaster and shipped to his Paris atelier on the Rue de Sevres, to ensure that his statue was lifelike. To replicate exactly the straining, bulging muscles of the horses depicted in the *Horse Tamers*, MacMonnies brought live horses to his studio as models. He cared about the park and donated a fountain of a small boy holding onto a slightly frenzied duck for the pool in the Vale of Cashmere. (It was later stolen from the park, but the Metropolitan Museum of Art has a replica.) MacMonnies also gave the park French artist Victor Peter's *Lioness with Cubs* (1899), which was originally placed at the Concert Grove.

A handsome bronze tablet of the Revolutionary War General Marquis de Lafayette in his colonial uniform by Daniel Chester French graces the Ninth Street entrance. French, known best for the exceedingly powerful 1920 statue of the former president at the Lincoln Memorial in Washington, D.C., is said to have worked with sculptor Augustus Lukeman on the poignant World War I memorial depicting a figure of the angel of death, made of bronze and holding a fallen American doughboy, which stands on the shore of the Lake, by the Concert Grove.

Two years after Lincoln was assassinated in 1865, a life-sized monument of the late president by Henry Kirke Brown was presented to the park and placed in the Plaza. It was the first like-ness of Lincoln in any city and today is located in the Concert Grove. Similarly, two years after President John F. Kennedy was assassinated in 1963, a bronze bust of Kennedy by Neil Estern adorned the Plaza. It was recently recast and is the only statue honoring Kennedy in New York City.

The first statue erected in memory of Abraham Lincoln was installed in 1869 at the Plaza. Today Lincoln overlooks the Lake from the Concert Grove. Photo, c. 1890s.

Gleaming like a Greek temple, the Peristyle is built on the site of an older shelter that overlooked the Parade Ground.

In the park's Imagination Playground children are mesmerized by this sculpture of Peter and his dog, Willie, from Ezra Jack Keats's stories. The tips of Peter's ears have been lovingly rubbed to a shine.

Early pieces of sculpture were often placed on pedestals to be appreciated by the viewer from below or from a certain distance. Robert Moses, New York Park Commissioner from 1934 to 1960, surrounded the ground-level *Lioness and Cubs* with five-foot-high fencing because children loved to touch it and slide down its sides, and then moved the sculpture to a more protected location at the zoo. Today the park's most recent works of sculpture, located in the Imagination Playground, are regarded differently. A bronze fountain in the shape of a dragon, designed in 1997 by the park's landscape architect, Christian Zimmerman, was created specifically for climbing. And a sculpture by Brooklyn artist Otto Neals, depicting characters from the books of children's author Ezra Jack Keats, is placed on a low ice age erratic, to be approached, touched, and conversed with directly by those for whom it was made.

Despite Olmsted's protests against the new monuments and other architectural elements, the influence of the City Beautiful movement in the park continued. The structure most reflective of this trend is McKim, Mead & White's Peristyle. At times called the Grecian Shelter, it is a gleaming Greek temple replica of white limestone. Its roof is supported by a series of Corinthian columns, and the interior ceiling is covered with Guastavino tiles. Erected on the site of an earlier Vaux-designed shelter that served, like the Peristyle, as an observation and judging stand for activities in the Parade Ground, the Peristyle may seem out of place to some in its setting of bucolic simplicity. It is nevertheless striking, as it stands with elegant grandeur overlooking the Parade Ground to the south and the Lake to the north.

A new Boathouse was built in 1905 on landfill at the east side of the Lullwater. Designed by Helmle, Huberty & Hudswell, it replaced an older boathouse that stretched across the base of Binnen Falls at the head of the Lullwater. Constructed of mat-glazed white terra-cotta, with a red-tile roof and an arcade of Tuscan columns, the Boathouse was inspired by the lower story of the sixteenth-century Library of St. Mark's in Venice by Jacopo Sansovino and is so eye-catching that it has often been used as a backdrop in films.

The firm of Helmle & Huberty is responsible for a number of distinctive buildings in Brooklyn, including the Hotel Bossert in Brooklyn Heights, the Spanish baroque St. Barbara's Roman Catholic Church in Bushwick, and the Greenpoint Savings Bank in Greenpoint, all of which have received landmark status. They also designed the 1910 Tennis House on a knoll on the west side of the Long Meadow, near the Ninth Street entrance—a site ironically selected by Olmsted in his capacity as consultant. While the building's Palladian style conflicts with the park's rustic design, the clash is obscured by a large group of trees and shrubs that largely hide the building and give it a somewhat mysterious quality. One glimpses its gray-white columns from a distance and upon approaching finds an elegant, vaulted court-yard that resembles an ancient Roman villa. The courtyard ceiling is supported by refined arches and pillars and is faced with russet-colored Guastavino tiles.

Other structures in the park by Helmle & Huberty include an addition to Litchfield Villa, an athletic and maintenance building at the Parade Ground, and an elegant comfort station at the Willink entrance, supported by Tuscan columns, faced with limestone and yellow brick, and embellished with a vaulted breezeway covered by dark green Guastavino tiles and a red-tile roof.

The comfort station, built in 1909, heralded the end of the neo-classical style in the park and was followed by the erection of several structures that were more in keeping with Olmsted and Vaux's original design. These included the Miniature Yacht Club House and a low-lying rustic shelter on the Peninsula.

Hidden by trees between the Picnic House and the Bandshell, the Tennis House, with its Palladian design, appears like an ancient Roman villa.

Both the Tennis House (left) and the Peristyle (right) are obscured by trees from the interior of the park. Only in the winter can you see their open, classical forms.

A Changing America

The impact of the City Beautiful movement on Prospect Park reflected ongoing rapid development throughout the borough. The Brooklyn Bridge was dedicated in 1883, facilitating access to New York City. Public transportation progressed from horse-drawn omnibuses to electric trolleys and elevated trains, making large swaths of Brooklyn available for development—though the growth was, at times, haphazard. Waves of new immigrants arrived, many from southern and eastern Europe. In 1898 the formerly independent Brooklyn became a borough of New York City, and construction of the Williamsburg and Manhattan Bridges over the East River soon followed. Electric lights illuminated the Plaza by 1909, and in 1920 the subway extended to it; new stations were later added at the Brooklyn Museum and at the park's Willink entrance. By the 1920s, property values soared, and the *New York Times* reported on new construction throughout Brooklyn as urban density increased. Stranahan's former mansion was demolished to erect a forty-unit apartment building. Single-family chateau-like houses on Park Slope's Gold Coast were overshadowed in 1924 by the fifteen-story apartment building at 9 Prospect Park West, near the park entrance.

With a larger Brooklyn population, the park attracted unimaginable crowds. During World War I, mass rallies were held there for such causes as eradicating the Red Menace and supporting the United States' troops in France. The acclaimed French actress Sarah Bernhardt stirred patriotic zeal when, in 1917, she addressed the fifty thousand people gathered at the Parade Ground to support the war effort. Ending her oration in French, she cried out from an open-touring car, "*Vive l'Amérique, vive les allies, vive la France.*"[57] A few days later, twenty thousand people gathered at the Parade Ground to recruit fighting men and show solidarity. French Army Marshal Joseph Joffre, considered the savior of France after the events of the Battle of the Marne, attended the dedication of French's Lafayette monument, driving to the ceremonies past American troops standing shoulder to shoulder, two men deep at Present Arms. During the celebration, rousing renditions of "La Marseillaise" and the "Star-Spangled Banner" were sung to great crowds of school children as they enthusiastically waved the Stars and Stripes and the French Tricolors. Just as the Americans had relied on the French during the American Revolution, the French now depended on their American allies.

The tragedy and irony of war, of course, is that former friends sometimes become new enemies. A mere five years earlier, in June 1912, German sailors from the battleship *Moltke* were given a royal tour of Prospect Park and wined and dined at the Waldorf-Astoria. They also visited Wall Street and Governors Island. When the war broke out in 1917, the Governors Island commandant, Colonel John C. F. Tillson, carried out the first act of war when he ordered the seizure of German ships docked at New York Harbor. Almost immediately, the Army stationed troops on the Long Meadow and erected an observation tower on Lookout Hill for searchlights. Boy Scouts

This monument to the Marquis de Lafayette was dedicated by French Army Marshall Joseph Joffre on May 10, 1917.

planted victory gardens in the park, while military baseball teams from the Brooklyn Navy Yard, including one managed by the legendary Casey Stengle, practiced at the Parade Ground in preparation for games against teams of the Atlantic fleet that put into Brooklyn.[58]

After the war, in June 1921, thirty-five thousand people lined the south shore of the Lake to attend the unveiling of the Prospect Park War Memorial, erected as a tribute to the twenty-five hundred Brooklyn men and women who died in the conflict. Throughout the year, even on the coldest winter days, visitors laid fresh flowers before the monument. For many parents it was the only grave they had for their boys. The park's southwest entrance was named after Emil J. Bartel and William J. Pritchard, close friends who grew up near the park and were killed in combat.

As the years passed, Prospect Park added even more layers to its original design. Where a remote wedge of the Adirondacks and the great lawn and lake at Stourhead in Wiltshire, England, were once replicated, signs of urbanization became visible. Rustic shelters that blended with the landscape gave way to imposing edifices that nature could barely conceal. Well-manicured and colorful gardens were planted in patches of meadow and woods, and ornate and imposing shrines took the place of nature's own monuments of majestic trees, precipitous ridges, and placid bodies of water. Man's vanity was supplanting nature's humility.

Despite these changes, Prospect Park retained its essential character. New buildings might have intruded on the margins of the Long Meadow, but they did not obstruct the view from the interior and were soon enveloped by foliage. The Ravine remained basically the same, as did the Lake—save for a few islands that were removed. Visitors still enjoyed unobstructed views of the Long Meadow and the Lake and found seclusion in the Ravine and the park's woodlands.

The original design accommodated the changes easily, but those who cared for the park had to remain vigilant. Prospect Park was under constant siege from proposed development. In 1915 a plan to turn a substantial portion of the park into a golf course was

The Long Meadow has remained largely unchanged since it was first created.

rejected, but a small course with nine sixty-by-sixty-foot greens and driving tees was built on the Peninsula. In 1925 the New York Park Conservation Association, representing forty-two civic associations, defeated a plan backed by New York Mayor John Hylan to build a college campus in the Deer Paddock. In 1928 the city's Transit Commission proposed running aboveground subway lines through the park that would have left it horribly disfigured. One line was to be routed into the park at Ninth Street, cutting through the hockey field—the site of the present-day Harmony Playground—and proceeding across the meadow to exit at Sixteenth Street. The other line was to run just inside the park along the Ninth Avenue wall to Fifteenth Street. In 1930 a new street was proposed to cut through Prospect Park, reflecting the growing threat of the automobile to the tranquility of the park.

Horseless carriages, or "electric carriages," seemed innocent enough when they first appeared around 1893 on the drives. A high-strung woman nearly fainted when she saw one moving along without a team of horses. "Something is the matter with me," she told her riding companion. "I see things strangely. That carriage there appears to be moving along without horses or driver—it's all a blank to me in front of the dashboard—what do you suppose it could mean?" She was greatly relieved to learn that she did not have "some impending affliction."[59] In the late 1800s the rare "buzzing, rumbling, choo chooing" machines remained playthings of the rich. George Jay Gould—son of Jay Gould, who was considered by some to be an archetypical robber baron—was one of the first to introduce automobiles in the park. He requested permission to use the drives after a polo match so he could avoid the exterior roads, which were in poor condition. The automobile gained official acceptance in 1899, when it was allowed in the park at a speed limit of eight miles per hour.

The main argument against automobiles was the same as it once was against bicycles: automobiles spooked horses and would cause an epidemic of runaways, serious injuries, and even deaths. It was also argued that cars were still experimental and broke down constantly. Within two years after cars were permitted within the park, auto races were held between gasoline, electric, and steam-powered cars. The competitions began with a parade that passed through Prospect Park on its way to the starting line at Ocean Parkway. The park would never be the same. Automobile traffic rose by 100 percent between 1904 and 1906, damaging roads that could previously go three years without repair—now they did not last a season. The dust could not be kept down, and the park's maintenance budgets were quickly devoured. By 1908 automobiles, especially the inexpensive Ford Model T (also called the Tin Lizzie), began to dominate the drives. From 1914 to 1916 the park's budget for plants and lawns was cut by 30 percent, while funds allocated for the drives, which were paved with macadam to avoid rutting the old gravel surfaces, increased by 50 percent. In 1924 the speed limit was raised to twenty miles per hour from fifteen, and during the next two years there were 622 auto accidents. To improve road safety in the park, traffic was made one-way, and shrubs and

overhanging limbs were cut back to ensure at least one hundred feet of unobstructed view for drivers. It was the beginning of a long struggle, not only about maintenance funding and the legitimacy of cars in the park, but also about the very basic notion of how Prospect Park should be experienced.

While park officials had some control over the use of automobiles, the arrival of the airplane was a challenge they could do little about. After World War I, planes were becoming familiar sights in Brooklyn. In 1927 aviator Charles A. Lindbergh took off on his solo trans-Atlantic flight to Paris from nearby Roosevelt Field, and on one occasion after his triumphant return, appeared at the Parade Ground to the welcome of two hundred thousand people. Just five months later, the Parade Ground filled with one hundred thousand expectant children and their parents awaiting Santa Claus's arrival in a biplane piloted by Clarence E. Chamberlain, the second man to fly across the Atlantic.[60] When the crowd spied a small black speck in the sky, a shout went up: "There he is!" The plane with the red-suited Santa approached, and he waved from the open rear cockpit as he circled several times and then landed "like a bird" in a great ring of people. It was, for children and adults, "a thrill you get once in a lifetime."[61] It was not long before planes regularly flew over the park on the approach to Glenn H. Curtiss Airport. The drone of low-flying aircraft was an intrusion that Olmsted and Vaux could never have imagined. The airport was later renamed LaGuardia Airport, after New York Mayor Fiorello La Guardia. The modern era had arrived.

A reception for Charles A. Lindbergh drew a huge crowd to the Parade Ground in 1927. Note the baseball diamonds in the rear.

Chapter Five

THE NEW DEAL
AND BEYOND

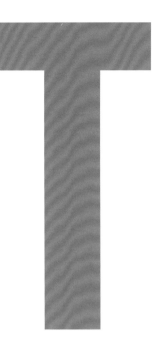

THE GREAT DEPRESSION, WHICH BEGAN IN 1929, meant hard times for Prospect Park, but it also brought an influx of visitors seeking escape from economic turmoil. Hizzoner Ed Koch, mayor of New York from 1979 to 1988, remembers with fondness the many good times he enjoyed in the park during the 1930s, even as it began to decline from lack of maintenance. "Gamboling in Prospect Park on weekends was wonderful," Koch recalled.[1] There were concerts, lazy picnics on the Long Meadow, and all those silly simians to mimic at the zoo. Many others similarly remember the pre–World War II park: it was their backyard, their carnival, and their theater.

Brooklyn architect Joseph Merz, who later became park curator in the 1970s, recalled how, as a teenager, he would look down with amusement from the Lullwater Bridge at the gridlock of colliding boats and their laughing occupants as they rowed their way to the Lake. Rowboats were available until midnight in the summertime and were festooned with lanterns to create a wonderfully romantic mood.

Merz called the Music Grove, the stand of trees adjacent to the Music Pagoda, "yesterday's Tanglewood."[2] Concert crowds would picnic there while listening to the Goldman Band on soft and fragrant summer evenings.[3] Twelve thousand people turned out when Mayor Fiorello La Guardia took up the baton in August 1934. Edwin Franko Goldman started his New York Military Band in 1911 and wrote more than one hundred marches, including "On the Mall" and "Hail Stranahan," many of which were played in Prospect Park. He also performed classical pieces for nearly sixty years, giving New Yorkers the opportunity to appreciate classical and popular music in a delightful, leisurely way outdoors.

By the mid-1930s, the beat of the big bands pulsed from the Picnic House after the city bowed to changing mores and permitted dancing in the park. Couples swamped the Picnic House dance the first night it took place, although only five hundred people were admitted—a thousand more clamored at the doors to swing to the music of Harry Raderman's band, the Gotham Boys. The event was so well attended that future dances took place at the adjacent parking lot—the brassy beat of the foxtrot and the jitterbug drew people from all over the borough. Dancing to the music of Benny Goodman and Cab Calloway became a part of the Prospect Park scene for many years, particularly after the Bandshell was erected in 1939. Violent crime was rare in those days, and it was considered safe to walk through the park at night after a dance or concert. Dodger fans also cut through the Ravine without fear on their way to and from nearby Ebbets Field.

On broiling summer nights entire families brought bedsheets to the park and slept by the Lake, under an arch, or beneath the stars on the Long Meadow. Slumbering in Prospect Park to escape the

PREVIOUS
The Vale of Cashmere was carefully restored by volunteers in the 1960s and 1970s.

138   PROSPECT PARK

nocturnal heat had been a summer tradition since the nineteenth century for the Brooklynites who were crammed into sweltering, sometimes windowless, apartments without air conditioning.

The whole park was a vast playground for young local boys who roamed it—some, like Merz, engaging in Soap Box Derby races down the macadam walkway from the summit of Breeze Hill to the Boathouse. They were also drawn to the Lake, skating on its frozen waters in winter and watching miniature-sailboat races in summer.

The park's more serious functions included serving as a political forum. Rallies drew patriots and veterans proclaiming loyalty to the United States, as well as Communists, Socialists, and their dissenters who railed against each other. In April 1936 Representative Hamilton Fish assailed President Franklin Roosevelt's New Deal policies at a rally at the Music Grove. At the same event, attended by an estimated five thousand, an official of the veterans-service organization American Legion described the proclamation for peace by Brooklyn College students as "nauseating in the extreme."[4] In May 1937 the seventeenth annual meeting of the Brooklyn Citizens' Patriotic May Day Celebration Committee drew thirteen thousand supporters to a park event. A local judicial officer, Surrogate George A. Wingate, was blunt in his nationalistic declarations: "We ought to get them Communists the hell out of here and do it pretty quick."[5]

While Prospect Park was a popular venue for a range of activities and brought joy to many, Depression-era crowds and declining budgets hastened the park's chronic deterioration. The lawns often went unmowed, cracked pavements were not repaired, trees died and were left to rot, and playgrounds became mud holes surrounded by chicken wire with a few swings and slides. The downward spiral finally halted in 1934 when Robert Moses was appointed New York City's park commissioner by newly elected reformist Fiorello La Guardia. Moses would reign for twenty-six years, and his power and influence in urban planning would be greater than that of any other man in the twentieth century. He had clearly defined ideas about the role of parks, which were at times contradictory. While he gave the impression that public parks were there for all the people—a favorite pastime of his was cruising through New York City in his black limousine looking for empty lots, especially in low-income neighborhoods, that could be turned into small parks and playgrounds—he also spent considerable amounts of money to add better facilities to outlying parks that were accessible only by private automobile. He believed that there should be a compromise between those who saw parks as places of beauty and those who wanted active recreation, but at the same time he considered parks without sports facilities as "undeveloped" and built numerous baseball diamonds, swimming pools, tennis courts, and ice-skating rinks.

Prior to arriving in New York City, Moses had been president of the State Park Commission, where he acquired thousands of acres for new parks. One prominent example is Jones Beach on Long Island, which has been called a "great country club for the common man."[6] He turned a sand bar into an elaborate seaside resort that included restaurants, a Venetian bell tower, and brick bathhouses. Later, as park commissioner, Moses set out to change and restructure the city's park department: he motorized the department's transport vehicles, still largely horse-drawn, and he immediately centralized control of the department under his exclusive authority. He had inherited a department with five borough commissioners and numerous local superintendents, all acting independently. On his first day, he fired them all. He also dismissed many unqualified patronage workers from the city's entrenched political machine, known for more than a century as Tammany Hall, including lifeguards who could not swim and "engineers" without high-school diplomas. He then put out a call for six hundred qualified engineers and architects to help rebuild and refurbish the city's parks. After the ad appeared, a line of unemployed applicants stretched eight blocks outside the Arsenal, the park department headquarters in Central Park. Some architects were hired on the spot, with the expectation that they would work fourteen-hour days and often weekends. The Arsenal's hallways were filled with cots and used as dormitories for the new staff. Demanding foremen pushed workers hard on three eight-hour shifts through a brutally cold winter to accomplish the seemingly impossible. All department employees were now under Moses's control.

Working for a supportive mayor, Moses took full advantage of generous funding provided by the federal government's New Deal. With incredible energy, he unleashed armies of Civil Works Administration (CWA)–funded personnel, who completed seventeen hundred projects in just a few months. The CWA was a temporary stimulus program established by the Roosevelt administration that provided funds to states and municipalities for public-works projects, including parks. The refurbishing work in Prospect Park was extensive: every bench was painted—from green to mocha—the lawns were reseeded, the bridle paths refurbished and reshaped, and the walks, drives, comfort stations, and drinking fountains were restored. Workmen removed hundreds of dead trees, planted thousands of saplings, and pruned and cut limbs to be used as fire logs by the needy. Moses also constructed several playgrounds and built a bike path along the park's western perimeter that has since been removed. The Works Progress Administration (WPA) workers even performed in a thirty-four-piece park-department band and produced plays and marionette shows.

Moses used his enormous influence to rewrite legislation so it allowed him to demolish any park structure without prior review. A replica of George Washington's home, Mount Vernon, erected on the Peninsula in 1932 to commemorate the bicentennial of his birth, was torn down in 1934. The reproduction had been controversial from the beginning. Nathan Straus Jr., president of the Park Association of New York and scion of the founder of the department store Abraham & Straus, had vehemently opposed the project, arguing that parks are for trees, grass, and flowers, not monuments. But it was nevertheless constructed, with wood siding, precut by

Sears Roebuck and Company, and painted, like the original, to simulate white stone blocks. By January 1933 it was in dire need of paint and its walks and gardens were filled with weeds.

Moses, who celebrated the new as beautiful and denounced the old as unworthy, ordered the demolition of several of Prospect Park's beloved iconic buildings that, with some foresight, could have been saved. The Dairy, which today would lend the park a sense of English charm, which Frederick Law Olmsted and Calvert Vaux so cherished, was torn down. A similar building, the Central Park Dairy, still exists in Central Park and is used as a handsome bookstore and information center.

The Concert Grove House also fell under the wrecker's ball despite a restaurateur's offer of $30,000 to turn it into a high-class restaurant with outdoor-eating facilities. Moses refused to cover the additional restoration costs, and so the park lost a festive gathering spot and an important example of Vaux's architecture. Somehow the Oriental Pavilion, adjacent to the Concert Grove House, was spared, but many of Vaux's distinctive rustic shelters were removed and his bridges replaced with utilitarian cement spans that had lead-pipe railings and chain-link fencing.

Moses, like the American public, considered the automobile as king, and during his administration cars became thoroughly folded into the fabric of Prospect Park. By the 1940s, as many as eighty thousand cars drove along the former carriageways on Sunday outings. To reduce accidents, Moses had portions of the drives straightened and removed several islands that had added beauty and foliage to the park's perimeter. He covered over grass with asphalt for parking lots behind the Music Pagoda in the Music Grove, as well as next to the Boathouse comfort station. Critics complained that the lots were disfiguring, just as the large parking area adjacent to Litchfield Villa was, which obliterated a lovely, tree-shaded swale that led into the Long Meadow. (The lots by the Music Pagoda and the Boathouse have since been restored to their original state.)

While many cherished buildings fell victim to Moses's rebuilding, he also added various structures to the park that were enthusiastically

Live music drew dancers to the
Bandshell in the 1950s.

received and that remain popular. The Bandshell, designed in 1939 by Aymar Embury II, who frequently worked with Moses, was erected on the old archery field that would later become the field-hockey grounds. Five ball fields were created on the southern end of the Long Meadow, including one framed with brick bleachers. Near the end of his tenure, in 1960, Moses also oversaw the planning of the Wollman Rink, which permitted outdoor skating everyday in winter.

The park commissioner's largest park project was the zoo, constructed in the former Deer Paddock, facing Flatbush Avenue. Olmsted and Vaux had first proposed a menagerie along Prospect Park West and Fifth Street on the park's perimeter. One was eventually built on Sullivan Hill and stocked with donated animals, including a bear given by former president Theodore Roosevelt. In 1914 seventy-five new animals were acquired from zoos in Great Britain, cast off because of the economic hardships brought on by World War I. When the ship docked after its trans-Atlantic voyage, a bear escaped and drove the tough longshoremen to the rafters above the pier. The menagerie was popular with park visitors, but it was inadequately funded and was generally in a dilapidated state, with unkempt grounds and cages that resembled shacks.

The zoo, opened in 1936, was designed by Embury and built with WPA funds and workers. The *New Yorker* magazine's architectural

critic Lewis Mumford praised the park's new facility: "From the stairs that lead down to the zoo, one can take in the plan at a glance. It is simple, logical, consistent, elegant, in a word all the things that the plan of the Central Park Zoo, unfortunately, is not." Mumford particularly commended "the moat of water at the bottom of the deer runs, the curve in the elephants' open air cages, and the absence of bars wherever possible."[7]

The zoo drew 2.2 million visitors its first year and began adding to its animal collection. The man responsible for assembling all of the new species was Al Smith, former New York governor and onetime presidential candidate. Because the city had no funds to stock the zoo during the depths of the Depression, Smith sought donations that included foxes from England, bears from Canada, and lions from Ethiopia. The zoo and the park also became a dumping ground for unwanted animals. Shortly after the new Central Park Zoo opened in 1935, Joe, an "imperious" male sea lion, was transferred to Prospect Park because his nocturnal barking disturbed the sleep of the influential Fifth Avenue residents. Jim, the polar bear, also arrived from Central Park, along with inbred and "deformed" sheep, cast off when Moses created the Tavern on the Green.[8] The sheep were let out to graze on the Long Meadow.

The New Deal financial bonanza was shortlived. Within six years the United States was at war, and public funds were not available for major capital projects and much-needed maintenance. When officials from Queens approached Moses about building a zoo in their borough in 1957, he replied that, absent another depression with New Deal–like funding, it would need to be underwritten with private donations.[9] His words were prescient: by the century's end, Prospect Park relied heavily on private funding for projects and programs.

World War II's Widespread Effects

When war was declared on December 8, 1941, Brooklyn scrambled to meet the crisis. German U-boats stalked shipping channels just off Gravesend and sank vessels within sight of the borough, and fighter planes flew over the city, taking off regularly from nearby Mitchel Field to guard against possible attacks. Mock air-raid drills were frequently held, but Brooklynites often failed to cooperate. Prospect Park was the only place in the borough where there were no blackout violations, but it was far from empty or quiet. During an air-raid drill on the night of July 7, 1942, the Pepsi Cola Band continued playing a medley of songs at the Music Pagoda as the blackout descended and the audience sang in accompaniment. Together they gave rousing renditions of "Hail, Hail, the Gang's All There," and "Let Me Call You Sweetheart."

All day and night the park was bustling with military activity. In December 1941 Battery C from Fort Totten set up antiaircraft guns and searchlights and stationed troops and sentries around Lookout Hill. Additional guns from the Sixty-Second Coast Artillery Battalion were positioned at the north end of the Long Meadow near Roosevelt Hill as well as along the east side path just beyond Endale Arch.

The clang and bang of dummy shells being loaded into the gun breeches during practice drills could be heard around the park. According to one account, Roosevelt Hill was the site of an underground ammunition-storage bunker that later became a playground when the troops departed. Children explored the bunker and played in the abandoned gun emplacements until they were filled in.[10]

Park Slope brownstones were turned into rooming houses as thousands of war workers poured into Brooklyn to manufacture everything from parachutes to gun clips. The USS *Arizona*, sunk at Pearl Harbor and now a memorial, and the USS *Missouri*, on whose foredeck the Japanese surrendered in Tokyo Bay in 1945, were both built at the Brooklyn Navy Yard. The yard employed more than seventy thousand people, who worked in shifts around the clock. Women who had previously been seamstresses became skilled welders and ship fitters. During their off-hours many of these uniformed men and women went to enjoy Prospect Park.

Baseball was a popular diversion for parkgoers around this time, as was horseback riding, which enjoyed a revival in the 1940s. A riding craze had previously swept Brooklyn in the 1880s, when on some days hundreds of equestrians filled the winding trails throughout the woodlands and along the southern Lake shore, often riding on connected bridle paths all the way to Coney Island and back during a single day's jaunt. Riding in those days was generally a pastime of the wealthy, who could afford proper attire and the considerable cost of maintaining a horse, but during the Depression and World War II, local stables made riding more affordable. The celebrated jockey Walter Blum earned money as a youngster shining shoes on Brooklyn's streets so he could ride in the park. Other children mucked out stalls at the numerous stables to pay for the hourly riding fare. Gangsters also enjoyed an occasional ride. The incendiary mobster Joey Gallo rode in Prospect Park and once became so angry with his temperamental steed that he jumped off and punched it in the nose.[11]

In the 1930s and 1940s there were numerous stables around Park Circle and behind Grand Army Plaza, including Black and White, Bates, Sea Lion, Little Gray Barn, and Prospect Park Stables. By the 1970s the number of riders had declined, and today only one stable remains—the Kensington Stables near Park Circle.

Postwar Brooklyn

When the war ended, an ironic twist to the nation's growing prosperity occurred in Brooklyn: here the end of the war brought decline. Veterans took advantage of the GI Bill, attended college, and found well-paying jobs elsewhere. Robert Makla, a lawyer who championed Prospect Park for many years after growing up in Park Slope and later became director of the Greensward Foundation, remembered the 1950s as the time when the streets began to empty and old residents left.[12] The vibrant life of the front stoop was displaced as people moved away or inside to air-conditioning and televisions that cast an eerie glow on every living-room ceiling.

OVERLEAF
Equestrians have experienced the park for more than 150 years.

Brooklynites gathered
at the Parade Ground to
protest the departure of the
Dodgers in 1957.

The nadir of Brooklyn's decline is often associated with the departure of the beloved Dodgers in 1957—just two years after the baseball team finally won the World Series by defeating its archenemy, the New York Yankees. To keep the Dodgers from leaving Brooklyn for Los Angeles, City Council President Abe Stark offered to build the team a new stadium at the Parade Ground, and Moses offered the 1939 New York World's Fair site in Flushing Meadow, Queens. But Walter O'Malley, the Dodgers's owner, wanted the rail yards around Atlantic Avenue and encouraged Moses to condemn the land by eminent domain as he had elsewhere for other projects. When O'Malley was denied, the Dodgers moved west.

"When the Dodgers left, they took the heart out of Brooklyn," said Howard Golden, Brooklyn-borough president from 1977 to 2001.[13] The team had unified Brooklyn. Cultural and social distinctions disappeared at Ebbets Field—everyone was just a Dodgers fan. O'Malley was responsible for a significant social breakthrough when he hired the first African American Major League Baseball player, Jackie Robinson, to man second base. Even non-Brooklynites remember legendary players such as Robinson, Pee Wee Reese, Duke Snyder, Gil Hodges, and Roy Campanella. Only a few remnants of that unusual and wonderful era remain: the home plate from Ebbets Field and several bleacher seats are displayed in the borough president's office.

The loss of the Dodgers was only the most obvious sign of the decline that was to continue during the following decades. The borough's industry was moving to the suburbs and to the south, where the land was aplenty and the labor cheap. New Jersey had room for expansion and easy connections to the new interstate-highway system. Brooklyn's wharves fell silent as goods were being loaded and unloaded in containers requiring only a crane and a handful of men rather than in large cargo nets by dozens of long-shoremen. The Navy left the Brooklyn Navy Yard, and the breweries left Brooklyn. The borough had been one of the nation's largest brewing centers, producing one-fifth of the country's beer in 1960. When Rheingold and Schaefer left in 1976, beer production in Brooklyn ceased for the next couple decades.

Symbolic too was the decline of the Montauk Club, the elegant brownstone-and-brick Venetian Gothic structure that overlooks Grand Army Plaza. Men dressed in striped trousers and cutaways used to enjoy sumptuous meals costing thousands of dollars there—women and wives were excluded. The facility opened its doors in the 1950s to families, and meals could be had for as little as $8. Grand mansions underwent similar transformations. For example, the Behr House on Pierrepont Street in Brooklyn Heights morphed from elegant homestead to hotel to rooming house to brothel, until it was saved when it became a Franciscan friary. The venerated Brooklyn Academy of Music almost became a tennis barn. Things would continue to get worse before they got better.

White middle-class families fled to new suburban developments, made possible by federally subsidized roads and Veterans

Administration loans restricted to the purchase of new houses. In the late nineteenth and early twentieth century, bridges were constructed to bring people into Brooklyn, but when the double-decked, twelve-lane Verrazano-Narrows Bridge was completed in 1964, people started to move out to Staten Island and New Jersey. There were many reasons to buy a house elsewhere: urban riots took place in Brooklyn in the 1960s; urban renewal was demolishing neighborhoods; redlining banks were limiting where they and the federal government would guarantee mortgages; and real estate agents—practicing what was known as "blockbusting"—were capitalizing on white residents' fears of minorities.

Crime became rampant in parts of Brooklyn, including Prospect Park, and the public demanded increased security. During the nineteenth century, crime in the park had mostly been restricted to acts of vandalism. In some cases bullies and "loafers," as they were called, tormented visitors. "Keepers" were hired to maintain order, but they were often retirees who were not able to control the problem. There was an instance of a gang of "half-grown roughs" swooping down on a children's picnic in the 1880s and stealing the entire picnic lunch; another one of thugs in the 1890s who subjected tennis players, particularly women, to taunts and insults.[14]

Crime in the mid-twentieth century, on the other hand, was serious and widespread. In 1950 teenage members of the Nits gang exchanged zip-gun fire with the Greene Avenue Stompers as by–standers dove for cover. Several hours later they reformed battle lines in Prospect Park on Payne Hill, known to gang members as Massacre Hill. A fifteen-year-old boy was shot in the head. It was not the first time gangs had battled in the park. On another occasion, toughs from South Brooklyn and Red Hook exchanged fire that killed an eighteen-year-old. Brooklyn had more gangs than any other borough, and gang members were armed with guns, lead pipes, bicycle chains, and switchblades.

Prospect Park's growing emptiness also provided the perfect cover for gangsters, who used the park as a meeting place, including members of Albert Anastasia's notorious Murder Inc., an assassination squad organized by the mob. Even spies made use of the park. The infamous Rudolph Ivanovich Abel transmitted U.S. defense secrets to the Russians in the 1950s on tiny dots of microfilm that he hid in hollowed-out coins and placed in prearranged drop sites as well as in a magnetic metal box stuck to a rarely used park gate.

In 1959 the park department stripped away the understory in the Ravine and in the vale in an attempt to deprive muggers of hiding places. This had little effect, however, since most hoodlums never hid in the bushes, and the loss of understory hastened the destruction of the landscape. The earth hardened, and rain cascaded down the hillsides preventing new growth, killing older trees, carving deep furrows in the hillsides, and silting up the streams. The sight of the devastation prompted Grace Lichtenstein of the *New York Times* to later write, "If Betty Smith were to write her famous novel today, she might call it 'A Tree Dies in Brooklyn.'"[15, 16]

Luckily, Prospect Park survived the trials of the 1950s, 1960s, and 1970s with occasional funding from the city for large projects. In 1959 the park department embarked on a six-year, $9 million face-lift—the first of its kind since the 1930s—to restore the park's buildings and grounds. "Maintenance crews are now giving Prospect Park its greatest overhauling since the 526 acre oasis was formally opened," reported the *New York World-Telegram and Sun*.[17] The work included the reconstruction of roadways, perimeter fences and walls, comfort stations, and the stone wall around the Lake, as well as the replacement or repair of broken benches and drinking fountains and the complete rewiring of the park.

The outdoor Wollman Rink was a popular new addition completed in 1961. It opened to great fanfare and a skating demonstration by Dick Button, the two-time Olympic gold medalist. As exciting as the rink was, it and its adjacent yellow and orange brick building were built on top of Music Island, which destroyed the century-old view of the Lake from the Concert Grove.

The Parade Ground also underwent reconditioning, and a new athletic building replaced the earlier structure by Helmle & Huberty. In the late 1960s the park received a $1.7 million federal grant to restore Litchfield Villa and the Boathouse as well as the Vale of Cashmere. This marked a new approach to landscape rehabilitation: the plan called for the vale to be restored to its original design, instead of being uprooted and replanted, as was convention.

Despite all the work in the late 1950s and early 1960s, the face-lift had little effect on the park's decline. Even while new construction took place, Prospect Park suffered from a lack of funds for maintenance, and the general landscape continued to deteriorate.

Preservation and the Park

Beginning in the early 1960s, however, public awareness of historic preservation grew, generated in part because of the announcement of the demolition of New York's Pennsylvania Station in 1961 and the publication of Jane Jacobs's groundbreaking book, *The Death and Life of American Cities*, the same year.[18] In it the urban activist argued in favor of renewing neighborhoods rather than tearing them down—the prevailing practice of postwar urban renewal, when whole neighborhoods were bulldozed and replaced with high-rises. Penn Station's demolition reflected this practice. Designed fifty years earlier by McKim, Mead & White, the station was modeled after the Baths of Caracalla and the Basilica of Constantine in ancient Rome. Penn Station was demolished in 1963 and its beautiful adornments hauled to the Meadowlands in New Jersey, which could then be called "the world's most elegant dump."[19] Outraged preservationists and architects rallied too late to stop Penn Station's destruction, but they succeeded in persuading the city to establish the New York City Landmark Preservation Commission in 1965. Brooklyn Heights immediately became New York City's first landmarked district, and a year later Congress passed the National Historic Preservation Act.

At Prospect Park a handful of concerned individuals stepped in to save the deteriorated Boathouse, which was slated for demolition in 1964. It was not the first time this elegant structure was threatened. The mayor's Art Commission had recommended that it be demolished in 1942, but it survived—undoubtedly because World War II diverted everyone's attention. Frank J. Helmle Jr., son of the architect; Joseph Mathieu, chairman of the Committee on Preservation of Historic Buildings; Governor Hugh Carey; City Council Majority Leader Tom Cuite; Makla; and Pulitzer Prize–winning poet Marianne Moore were among those who met with Park Commissioner Newbold Morris to save the building from the Art Commission. Mumford joined the chorus: "Save Prospect Park boathouse," he implored. "Now that Pennsylvania Station is gone no good building will be safe unless a firm stand is taken against this commercial vandalism. The city must not be treated as a disposable container."[20]

Intervention came just in time. Bulldozers were set to turn the Boathouse into rubble the day after the meeting. Not only was the structure saved, it was declared a city landmark a year later. The fight to preserve the Boathouse was the first time people organized to battle against the tearing down of an important park structure, setting a much-needed precedent. In addition to the Boathouse, the Peristyle was granted landmark status to prevent its razing, which had been planned in the mid-1960s.

The Camperdown elm near the Boathouse

Historically important natural elements of the landscape were not overlooked as preservationists found their cause in the park. Notably, an ailing Camperdown elm just down the path from the Boathouse was also saved. Planted in 1872, it needed bracing and the eighteen cavities in its gnarled limbs required immediate attention. Called a "singularly curious elm" by Olmsted and Vaux, the Camperdown was a mutation of a Scotch elm (which grows along the ground rather than upward) and was a popular garden feature of that era. The elm in Prospect Park was taken from a tree at Camperdown House in Dundee, Scotland, and grafted onto a regular Scotch elm rootstock that had been donated by A. G. Burgus. The park department had no plans to protect it until Moore, in 1966, rallied support with her poem "The Camperdown Elm," which appeared in the *New Yorker*. Among the poem's most compelling lines are:

> *props are needed and tree food. It is*
> *Still leafing: still there. Mortal though*
> *We must save it. It is our*
> *Crowning curio.*[21]

Moore's appeal for donations in a letter to the *New York Times* helped save the elm. "I morbidly thought: my enterprise seemed doomed to fail, but No!" She later wrote, "Life is worth living when people have hearts."[22] This was a small but important victory on the long road to restoring Prospect Park. The Camperdown elm survives to this day.

Earlier demolitions of the Dairy and the Concert Grove House were huge, but silent, losses. Only recently, during the 2012 reconstruction of Music Island, workers discovered evidence of other demolitions made by the Moses administration in 1960, the remains of which became fill for the construction of Wollman Rink. During work on Lakeside in 2012, carved stone copings and posts that had formed the base of a wrought-iron fence in the Concert Grove were uncovered. Some of these remains, along with two partially recovered decorative stone fountains, were reconditioned and reused. They are poignant reminders of the beauty of a bygone era. Perhaps the remains of the Dairy are, in fact, still buried in the park.

Increasing Support for the Park

In the latter part of the 1960s, public efforts on behalf of the park became more organized. In anticipation of the 1966 centennial celebration of the park's opening, a group of Brooklyn residents formed the Greensward Foundation, led by Makla, to push back against municipal and public indifference to preservation. Architect-historian Clay Lancaster headed the Friends of Prospect Park, a subgroup of the foundation; the architecture critic Henry Hope Reed directed the Friends of Central Park, another subgroup; Moore was titular foundation head.

The park's plight was taken up by Mayor John Lindsay, who declared Prospect Park "one of the most pastoral and naturalistic, man-made parks in the United States," while noting the insults that had been made to its integrity: "historic structures altered or destroyed, the finest trees cut down, its beautiful gardens turned into swamps, magnificent statuary vandalized, walks and bridges shattered, and the erection of ugly and makeshift structures."[23] Lindsay appointed Thomas P. F. Hoving, curator of the Cloisters, a center of medieval art at the Metropolitan Museum of Art, as park commissioner in January 1966. Remembered as a master of "happenings" in Central Park and a proponent of small, neighborhood "vest-pocket parks," Hoving was emphatic about protecting Prospect Park, because he believed that "Prospect Park is the greatest naturalistic manmade park in the world with Central Park a close second."[24] With three degrees in art and architecture from Princeton University, Hoving saw both parks as "works of art, as a painting or sculpture," and argued for their preservation: "Just as one would not take Mr. Clean and a wire brush to tamper with a great masterpiece one must not tamper in an unwarranted fashion in a great park."[25]

Hoving immediately appointed curators—voluntary park directors without authority or funding—for Prospect and Central Parks. Lancaster, the curator of Prospect Park, was a staunch defender of Olmsted and Vaux's original design. He led walking tours through the park, penned a guidebook full of architectural details, and took controversial stands—including a call to demolish Wollman Rink and the Bandshell, which he called some of the park's "worst features now existing."[26, 27]

Troubled Leadership in a New Era

Centennial ceremonies for Prospect Park in 1966 were extensive and included a parade of antique cars, high-wheeled bicycles, and horse-drawn carriages, as well as many participants in period costumes. The Music Pagoda served as a reviewing stand, and Miss Prospect Park cut a mammoth birthday cake. The celebration continued all summer, with concerts, operas, and dance performances, but the festivities did little to reverse the ongoing decline.

As the park moved into its second century, new volunteer advocates emerged, including William Novak and M. M. "Dickey" Graff, who crusaded for a safer, cleaner, and better-maintained park. In a letter to the *New York Times*, Graff called for a decentralization of the park department's authority "so those who use the parks have some control over it." She also accused Lindsay of failing to implement his proposals to restore the park and called his record a "total disaster."[28] Knowing that they lacked the resources to deal with all of the park's problems, the volunteers focused on restoring the overgrown and deteriorated Vale of Cashmere to its former beauty and glory. They weeded, pruned, replanted, picked up litter, cleared silt and phragmites—giant invasive reeds with six-foot-deep root systems—from the pools, and even installed a bubbling fountain to recirculate the water. The effort lasted a decade, but the best of intentions were still insufficient. The vale needed too much work.

Officials gather for Prospect Park's centennial anniversary. Seen here seated from left to right are Park Commissioner Thomas P. F. Hoving, Mayor John Lindsay, Borough President Abe Stark, and former commissioner Robert Moses at the far right.

One of the least known sections
of the park, the vale is one of its
most beautiful, tucked away just off
the Long Meadow.

The park department had hoped that Lancaster's efforts as curator would improve the park, but he had his own vision that often ran counter to department policy. For example, he vehemently opposed the park department's plan to construct a children's farm next to the zoo. The farm, eventually built, was created to bring a slice of rural life to urban children, with a cow, chickens, ducks, and pigs. Lancaster was dismissed in 1967, perhaps because of the controversy surrounding this issue.

Donald Simon, a former park department employee, was appointed the next curator of Prospect Park by Park Commissioner August Heckscher. (Hoving had left to become director of the Metropolitan Museum of Art from 1967 to 1977.) Simon had a few successes, such as persuading the city transportation department to stop straightening the drives for automobile traffic. But he faced nearly insurmountable problems. Much of the park's maintenance equipment was inoperable. A bulldozer sat idle, because the city could not afford a simple $500 part. Bucket trucks for tree pruning were out of commission, so workers manually snipped off dead tree branches until "they limbed so many they looked like telephone poles," Simon recalled.[29]

After Simon left in 1974, architects Joseph and Mary Merz became cocurators. Joseph had also been a former consultant to the National Park Service. Like the curators before them, they had limited resources: few tools, little financial assistance, and a mere handful of volunteers. The original park structures continued to deteriorate. Reviving Prospect Park seemed like a hopeless and never-ending task, and after two years the Merzes resigned.

The following years saw little improvement. Indeed, the park seemed to be under attack: the attempted theft of the three-hundred-pound bust of John Howard Payne was among the assaults. Three men, using chisels and axes, removed the bust from its granite pedestal and rolled it downhill, but their plans were thwarted by a police officer waiting at the bottom. The Peristyle's copper gutters were stolen, causing the columns and capitols to crack and the Guastavino ceiling tiles to buckle. Vandals wrecked the Tennis House. In just the first half of 1974, 140 people, mostly bikers, were mugged in or near the park. A year later, police on scooters escorted bicyclists on the drives, conjuring images of shotgun-toting stagecoach guards in the Wild West. "My God, has it come to this, that we need a wagon train sort of thing?" one cyclist complained.[30] Compounding the problems was a 25 percent reduction in the police force safeguarding the park.

"This park has been manhandled," the *New York Times* reported in 1973. "Old fashioned black iron lampposts, the kind with lacy iron veils to protect the glass, decapitated....The Nethermead Arches and Meadow Port [*sic*] Arches and park benches sprayed with Everykid's name...January ponds are iced litter traps....Beer cans, pop cans, gum wrappers, lollipop sticks, flying scraps of *Sunday Times*. The undertrash buries the underbrush in some of the thickets."[31] It was no wonder that, in 1974, 44 percent of New Yorkers polled by the marketing and research firm Daniel Yankelovich Inc. warned everyone to stay away from Prospect Park.[32]

The conditions in the neighborhoods around the park were equally bad. "It is a terrible thing to be beset by fear," Moore said as she left her beloved Brooklyn after thirty-eight years to move to a safer Greenwich Village.[33] While there was evidence that by the 1970s the white flight had slowed as young professionals, induced by the low prices, moved to Park Slope—a four-story brownstone could be as little as $40,000—landlords around the park still abandoned buildings. The city demolished many structures, leaving gaping holes in neighborhoods and encouraging further decline.

In the mid- and late 1970s a group of concerned Park Slope residents, mostly stay-at-home moms, pressured public officials to clean up the park after children contracted impetigo in contaminated sand at the Third Street Playground. When it was closed for renovation, families visited the Garfield Play Lot and were equally appalled by the conditions there. Children vied with rats for space in the sandboxes.

Local resident Barbara McTiernan, who was later involved with the Prospect Park Alliance, organized community members through the Park Slope Civic Council to help improve these conditions, specifically focusing on the Third Street Playground. In spite of these efforts, it would take until the end of the decade, after Park Commissioner Gordon Davis met with the group and promised action, for the situation to improve.

During the 1960s and 1970s, management of the park system was consistently fragmented and lacking in continuity. There was little supervision, and apathy reigned because of the constant change of commissioners. At the same time, New York simply did not have the financial resources to maintain its parks. The city's plight was in fact so severe that Mayor Abraham Beame asked President Gerald Ford for federal assistance in 1975, but the response was swift and blunt, summed up in a huge headline on the front page of the *Daily News*: "Ford to City: Drop Dead."[34] As a result, the city slashed the park budget by more than $40 million, a 60 percent reduction in expenditures. From 1975 to 1976, the capital-improvements budget for park renovations and new structures decreased from $24 million to $5 million. Park Commissioner Martin Lang noted, "We have taken off the fat and we are into muscle and bone."[35]

Then an event occurred that jolted the Brooklyn community. The statue of Columbia fell from her chariot atop the Soldiers and Sailors Memorial Arch in Grand Army Plaza. She had reigned from the arch for more than three-quarters of a century until the blustery night of October 9, 1976, when a fierce storm lashed New York City. The gale snapped her rusted stanchions and slammed her on her back as she dangled seventy feet above the plaza. Her disgrace would become a turning point for Prospect Park.

Chapter Six

RECLAIMED AND RESTORED

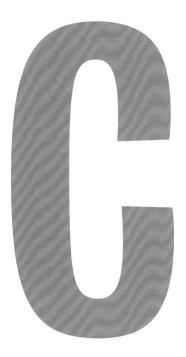

COLUMBIA WAS THE SYMBOLIC EMBODIMENT of nineteenth-century America as much as Uncle Sam is today. Sculpted by Frederick MacMonnies, she was placed atop the Soldiers and Sailors Memorial Arch with great fanfare in 1898. Olympian in pose, sword clutched tightly in her left hand and a signum-topped staff in her right, Columbia stood erect in her chariot, flanked on either side by a laurel-crowned, winged Victory. Like a conquering general of antiquity, she rode triumphantly in her four-horse quadriga.

Columbia was a fixture at Grand Army Plaza for seventy-eight years as the guardian of the park's entrance.[1] From her post she peered over the Long Meadow into the wooded ridges of the Vale of Cashmere and Battle Pass. She witnessed the comings and goings of presidents, generals, governors, mayors, and throngs of Brooklynites seeking a pleasurable outing in the park. During her watch, horse-drawn carriages gave way to motor cars, the clang and grind of electrified trolleys became the fumy rumble of buses, and the cries of birds were drowned out by the drone of LaGuardia Airport–bound planes.

After she toppled from her perch during the storm in 1976, the dangling Columbia was safely secured by New York City firemen so she would not fall, but to passing New Yorkers who looked up and saw this precariously hanging lady, she epitomized the ills plaguing the city and Prospect Park. Auspiciously, however, her fate roused people to action and heralded the park's rejuvenation, which continues to this day. "If she had not fallen, we would not be in a position to know how much work needed to be done here," proclaimed Mayor Ed Koch.[2] With Gotham nearly bankrupt, its middle classes fleeing to the suburbs, and its infrastructure decaying, Koch struggled to restore the city's fiscal health.

The political climate changed in 1977 when Brooklyn native Howard Golden became president of the borough and immediately began to rally its citizens, businesses, and community groups. "The idea was to build up the spirit; we started a pride movement to get all the forces together," Golden recalled.[3] His new slogan became "Brooklyn, A Nice Place to Visit. A Great Place to Live." Prospect Park, in particular, was a special place for Golden. Here he and fellow Brooklynites could escape from the city's hustle and bustle, breathe clean air, and enjoy the countryside. (As a boy Golden had played ball on the Parade Ground athletic fields.) In his new role, he became the park's greatest benefactor, funding at least $110 million for park projects during his twenty-four years in office. Among the many early projects he spearheaded were Celebrate Brooklyn!, a summer festival for the performing arts, which he launched in 1979 with his executive assistant Harvey Schultz, as well as the restoration of the Prospect Park Bandshell for use as Celebrate Brooklyn!'s venue in 1984.

The reinstallment of Columbia to her chariot in the fall of 1980 heralded a major infusion of capital funds by Mayor Ed Koch to improve the park.

PREVIOUS
Music Island was restored to its original beauty in 2012.

Golden had the support of Brooklyn Councilman Tom Cuite, New York's powerful city council majority leader, who controlled virtually every city public-works project. Golden and Cuite were the driving forces behind the park's revival. Crucially, Golden would see that funds were available to pursue a 1979 Prospect Park Preservation Plan.

With the turn of a new decade, on January 4, 1980, Prospect Park's fortunes received a powerful boost when Koch and Golden announced a major capital grant to help fund this plan. The park administration would receive $10 million to refurbish the Litchfield Villa Annex; to restore the Picnic House, the Boathouse, and the Tennis House; and to undertake a study to rebuild the Oriental Pavilion. The grant also specified the development of a list of priorities for restoration of the Ravine and the Long Meadow. The first orders of business, however, were the restoration of the park's buildings and convincing people to return to Prospect Park. "I cannot think of a better way for the Mayor to begin the New Year and a new decade," Koch declared at a gathering in Grand Army Plaza where he announced the funding.[4] After a champagne toast, he ascended the circular staircase to the top of the Memorial Arch, while Golden waxed poetic and quoted Moore: "Beauty is everlasting and dust is for a time." Prospect Park, he said, would no longer be forgotten.[5]

Responsibility for implementing the plan fell to Park Commissioner Gordon Davis. Although he lacked the employees and the money to accomplish the task, he had a vision of a rejuvenated Prospect Park and, following a string of five short-term park commissioners in a mere five years, was ready to force change in the department. He wanted to demonstrate to the public that the city had not forgotten its parks, and he appeared regularly on TV to send this message—he was filmed while cleaning up storm damage, cuddling baby sea lions in the parks' zoos, and even eradicating a hornet's nest dressed in beekeeper's attire.

Davis was a master of improvisation. In 1979 he hired twenty urban-park rangers, outfitted them in snappy National Park Service–type uniforms with Smokey-the-Bear hats, and assigned them to Central, Prospect, and Van Cortland Parks. "We recruited people who would bring a new perspective to the Park—not traditional park employees, but people with a fresh unfettered view," Davis said.[6] The rangers proved invaluable to the revival of Prospect Park, particularly in providing a sense of security and in offering educational and outreach programs.

Davis decentralized the ossified department bureaucracy and motivated workers by appointing autonomous borough park commissioners and independent administrators to run Central and Prospect Parks. He hired Elizabeth Barlow to become Central Park administrator and encouraged her to create the Central Park Conservancy, a public-private partnership whose mission was to raise private funds to supplement public monies for park maintenance and improvements. This new model would prove its worth by raising millions of dollars in its first few years.

Columbia and her quadriga have overlooked the park for a century and now watch over a thriving green market every Saturday.

In 1980 Mayor Koch appointed Tupper Thomas to be Prospect Park's first administrator.

Shortly thereafter, Davis hired Tupper Thomas as the Prospect Park administrator. Thomas, with an ebullient personality, was worldly, tough, and smart. She had run the Manhattan Urban Renewal program before pursuing a master's degree in urban planning from New York's Pratt Institute. She had experience in city government and politics, and was involved in community-organizing activities in Crown Heights—she knew Brooklyn better than Davis. The red-headed Midwesterner, who became known simply as Tupper, remained in office for thirty-one years and impacted the development of Prospect Park as much as anyone who had come before. Her tenure was longer than James Stranahan's by nearly a decade and longer even than that of Robert Moses. Years after she became Prospect Park administrator, Davis reflected on Tupper's abilities: "Tupper…knew how to get the most and best out of people. This wasn't just true of people with professional skills it was true throughout the community. Prospect Park needed someone who understood people…someone people would trust. Tupper had this gift that there wasn't anybody she couldn't relate to in some effective or positive way. Tupper has the ability to reach out to an ordinary Joe and establish a trust, which is a gift."[7]

In retrospect, these skills were crucial, as the job Thomas and her team faced at the outset was monumental. No one used Prospect Park except dog walkers, thugs, joggers—who thought they could outrun muggers—and bicyclists, who often rode with police-escorted convoys. Children played in the park only until dusk, when they fled in fear of harm. Even volunteers risked being mugged, and sometimes were. Crime and the fear of crime were so great that the number of annual visitors had dropped to 1.7 million in 1980, the lowest in a century.

The graffiti covering the Bandshell was emblematic of the park's derelict condition. The *New York Times* called it "a sorry symbol of neglect….The rundown structure seemed to deserve the graffiti that stained it and the undrained pools of water that surrounded it each spring."[8] The paved apron in front of the stage doubled as a makeshift roller hockey rink for neighborhood kids. When the players learned that the Bandshell was to be refurbished in 1982, they retaliated by setting fire to a temporary stage extension, then yanked it down. Throughout the early 1980s vandalism ran rampant in the park.

All of the park's buildings were closed to the public except the Picnic House, which served two days a week as a men's senior citizen center. The Tennis House was in shambles, and the restored Boathouse had again fallen into disrepair—instead of serving as a restaurant as intended after the renovation, it was closed to the public and functioned as a glass-recycling center. The Oriental Pavilion was a burned-out shell at the Concert Grove, with the fire's source—a brick hot-dog stand—still remaining. The park's bridges and arches needed repair, its playgrounds were filthy, benches were splintered, and many of the streetlights were shot out. Hardly any activities were scheduled for children or adults due to the fear of crime. Celebrate Brooklyn! was the only organization that offered programming.

There were no gardeners or horticulturalists maintaining Prospect Park when Thomas took office. The park staff—of more than one hundred—was leaderless, unresponsive, and unmotivated and limited by archaic work rules. Almost no one worked weekends, and litter lay scattered about until it was picked up midweek. An outside consultant reported that workers operated at 31 percent of capacity.

Dog walkers were among the only people who used the park in the late 1970s and early 1980s. Today's dogs are free to romp in the early mornings and evenings.

The New York Philharmonic performances are hugely popular among park visitors.

As administrator, Thomas had little power to effect immediate change, but with her usual optimism, she was determined to make a difference by setting a positive example. While supervising maintenance work on the Bandshell, for instance, which was flooded after a rainstorm, she asked the crew to open the clogged drain in front of the stage. When the workers replied that it was not their job, Thomas waded into waist-deep water, held her nose, and went underwater to pull out a wad of leaves. The startled crew hurried to help.

Thomas began assembling a qualified staff, and Davis assigned her an experienced park manager, Pat Pomposello, who understood Thomas's objectives and helped her sidestep rigid department rules and lines of authority. Pomposello was a pivotal and unheralded figure in the park's revival and later became the first chief of operations in the Queens parks system. But even with Pomposello's help, Thomas had a difficult time at the beginning. Workers initially resisted a woman supervisor and she was insulted by employees, some of whom expressed their resentment by dumping bags of garbage on the park drives.

Motivating the workforce was one challenge; getting people to return to the park was another. Thomas learned that most permit applications for public events were rejected by the park's administration, so she assumed this responsibility in order to encourage park use. Necessarily, this effort included tackling the issue of crime. Although there were "fewer incidents of crime in Prospect Park…than in any other area of the city," as New York City Police Commissioner Michael Murphy noted in 1964, "when something does occur, it gets the headlines because it happened in the Park."[9] In 1979 residential areas around the park were hazardous, and the park seemed more threatening than the street because of misleading news reports and blaring headlines such as "Woman Mugged *Near* Park" or "Man Shot *Near* Prospect Park." Thomas urged reporters and editors to be accurate when reporting crime and offered them tours to demonstrate the progress being made in the park.

Councilman Cuite also played a significant role by bolstering law enforcement. The park fell between precinct lines and police coverage was fragmented, but through Cuite's efforts patrols were coordinated. He also was instrumental in creating a police-task group and an auxiliary police force that patrolled Prospect Park. "The auxiliary police force was a really big thing for us because it got the cops involved in the park," Thomas recalled. "There was the perception of safety with blue uniforms all over the park and at activities." In fact, crime declined in the park in the 1980s while it continued to climb in New York City overall.

To entice people back to Prospect Park, Thomas immediately began promoting and developing annual events. A Harry Chapin concert was held in the Long Meadow—with the hope that it would appeal to thousands—but only three hundred people attended the event. Thomas heavily advertised the New York Philharmonic and the Metropolitan Opera performances that had occurred annually for more than a decade in the park, but which had recently had a low turnout. In December 1980 Prospect Park held a fireworks display on New Year's Eve over the north end of the Long Meadow, with free hot cider and jazz for spectators. A few hundred people showed up— today the same event draws thousands. The programs were promoted in a quarterly newsletter of upcoming events, which was published and distributed around Brooklyn.

The Bandshell, a venue that has accommodated the longest running summer music festival in New York, Celebrate Brooklyn! (begun in 1979), was extensively renovated by the parks department in 1984, along with the adjacent playground. Large parts of the stage were rebuilt and expanded, and drainage problems were remedied. The formerly destructive roller-hockey players had been successfully convinced to help create a responsible ice-hockey group at Wollman Rink.

The Halloween Pumpkin Festival, developed together with the urban-park rangers, was another early effort by Thomas to draw visitors to the park. Several hundred parents and children showed up in 1981, when it was held in the Picnic House. It was significantly expanded in subsequent years by the urban-park rangers, especially Rick Garcia, known as Ranger Rick, who provided artistic direction and played a major role in its success. Included was a haunted walk beginning at the Nethermead Arches, where dry ice produced a frightening, drifting miasma, inducing spine-chilling screams that echoed

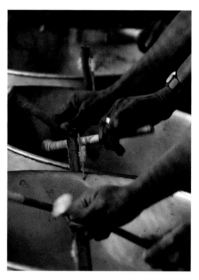

Music has always played a large role in Prospect Park.

Volunteers work hard
on costumes, makeup, and
props for the park's annual
Haunted Walk.

through the arches. Suddenly the cloaked and faceless grim reaper burst through the fog. Vampira sat bolt upright in her coffin, beckoning children with her finger as Dracula hissed at her side. Ranger Rick, attired and mounted as the Headless Horseman, thundered up and down the bridle path across the Ambergill, the stream running through the Ravine. Macabre figures jumped out of leaf-covered warrens, and a wet-suited apparition crawled from the watercourse as children crossed the Esdale Bridge. The children then made their way through the Ravine to Ambergill Falls and up the steps toward the old Elephant House, where strange sounds blared, while in a nearby clearing headless figures flailed away with real swords that lopped off fake limbs. One duel became so animated that a Kings County Shakespeare actress was accidentally stabbed and wound up in the hospital—but only after she finished her performance. Today, Halloween festivities take place on Lookout Hill, where the grim reaper still patrols, ghouls and goblins spring from a haunted house, victims are guillotined, and a loud sound system emits screeches and howls.

The core of Thomas's team in the early 1980s was the dozen or so urban-park rangers and six horse-mounted rangers, all of whom provided security and a friendly presence in the park. When Brooklyn-born Joseph Papp invited Shakespeare & Company to perform *Twelfth Night* at the Music Pagoda in 1982, the rangers led theatergoers through the meadows and woods to the Nethermead and remained on duty as protecting sentinels. The rangers were involved in numerous park activities, but they focused particularly on those

for children and youths, such as programs that aimed at revealing nature's wonders. Many rangers developed areas of specialty: Kevin Jeffrey conducted bird walks; other rangers specialized in pond life or trees. Ranger Rick was a beekeeper and lectured about bees. When giving talks he often covered his head with a pheromone to attract them—once a swarm went rogue, and Ranger Rick had to douse himself with water. After his death, the grounds of the old Elephant House on Sullivan Hill, the site of the original zoo and where he kept his bees, was named Rick's Place in his honor.

Thomas and the rangers also reinstated previously successful events that had been discontinued because of the park's decline—one example was the Macy's catch-and-release fishing contest, funded by the Abraham & Straus department store in the 1940s but canceled in 1979. Another was Eeyore's Birthday Party, during which a donkey—named after the stuffed gray donkey in A. A. Milne's *Winnie the Pooh*—leads a procession of children and parents from the zoo to the nearby Children's Farm for an afternoon of family-friendly activities. New programs spearheaded by Thomas included Volunteer Days, when the public could participate in cleaning up litter, and the biannual Art in the Arch event, started in 1984, during which works from various artists were displayed in and around the Memorial Arch.

Along with John Muir, director of the Prospect Park Environmental Center (PPEC), Thomas encouraged officials at nearby schools to establish field trips to the park to study nature. PPEC, later renamed the Brooklyn Center for the Urban Environment, produced several curricula, including "Discover a Park, Discover a City" and "Guide to Birds for the Park." This was the beginning of a long-term commitment to educating elementary and high-school students about environmental preservation and, in so doing, protecting the park.

A major goal of all of these outreach programs was to encourage greater ethnic and cultural integration. Brooklyn's demographics had changed dramatically since the 1960s, as thousands of immigrants

LEFT
Participants in the annual Abraham & Straus Fishing Contest, 1952

RIGHT
Catch-and-release fishing is still a popular activity in the park today.

arrived, giving a contemporary meaning to the Statue of Liberty's inscription, "Give me your tired and your poor," penned by Brooklyn's Emma Lazarus. The borough has always been known for its diversity. The Dutch, English, Irish, Germans, Italians, southern Europeans, Poles, and Scandinavians, who had immigrated earlier, were joined by Russians, Ukrainians, and Puerto Ricans in the twentieth century. Large numbers of African Americans moved in from the South during what is called the Great Migration, and even more immigrants came from the Caribbean Islands. The ethnic mix of the neighborhood changed further when new immigration laws adopted in 1965 and in 1985 brought in more Asians, Africans, and Latinos. Today 33 percent of Brooklyn's population is foreign born.[10]

So diverse was the borough that by the 1980s many whites felt outnumbered and were reluctant to use Prospect Park. African Americans tended to congregate on the park's east side near their own neighborhoods, Pakistanis would gather on the south, while whites and Latinos assembled in the Long Meadow because of its proximity to Park Slope and adjacent areas. Committed to Olmsted and Vaux's original design, which set out to usher people through the whole park, Thomas and her administration sought greater integration among the ethnic groups by encouraging everyone to use the entire grounds.

Today, immigrants from around the world embrace Prospect Park, and the diversity of events taking place there, such as a Haitian market, a Mexican fair, a Creole-reggae family fete, and a Chinese festival featuring choruses from Beijing and Canton, reflects the heterogeneity of the community.

Fund-raising and the Prospect Park Alliance

Raising money to sustain the park was a critical aspect of Thomas's position. While the largest funding source was the city government, private support for the park became increasingly important. By 1985 Prospect Park was receiving $250,000 annually from foundations, including grants from the J. M. Kaplan Fund, the New York Community Trust, and the Vincent Astor Foundation. Soon after she took office, Thomas began to plan the establishment of the Prospect Park Alliance to help in this fund-raising effort. As a counterpart to the Central Park Conservancy, the Alliance was envisioned as an autonomous public-private partnership that would manage the park, raise funds for restoration, and expand programming. The Central Park Conservancy was already proving successful and had completed several projects that would have been difficult to undertake without private support. A similarly productive Prospect Park Alliance would insulate the park from economic downturns and become the vehicle through which the park could foster stewardship and sustainability.

Although the Alliance was organized as a nonprofit in 1985, it was not formally launched until April 6, 1987, with trust and estates lawyer Henry "Terry" Christensen III serving as board chairman. The organization successfully raised funds from private grants and donations and, like the Central Park Conservancy, established an endowment. But it had few of the advantages of the Conservancy.

Central Park, known worldwide, is surrounded by top-end luxury real estate, some of the world's wealthiest people, and corporations willing to lavish huge contributions on its buildings and grounds. Prospect Park in the late 1980s, by contrast, was encircled by low-income neighborhoods with shuttered buildings, and Park Slope was only just beginning to attract professionals who could contribute materially to the park. In this landscape the Alliance began as a modest organization, with a small staff whose members performed multiple roles, sometimes even acting as concessionaires on weekends, peddling ice cream and sodas from the back of pickup trucks, and handing out trash bags to encourage people to clean up. A major component of the Alliance is the Community Committee, Com Com, which was formed to represent the diverse and changing community around the park that has a vested interest in its sustainability.[11]

The Alliance's first undertaking was the restoration of the Carousel, which had been closed since 1983. The existing Carousel was in fact the park's third. The original was built in 1874 at the Rose Garden and moved to the West Woods in 1885. When it burned down, it was replaced by a second Carousel, which, in 1935, also burned down. The third, and present, Carousel opened in 1952 and is a composite of two Coney Island merry-go-rounds built around 1912. The wooden animals and figures, including fifty-one life-size horses, one lion, one giraffe, and two chariots, were crafted by Charles Carmel, a noted Russian-born carver and master of the Coney Island style of horses with "flaring nostrils and prancing attitudes."[12] The Carousel closed in 1971 for renovations and reopened in 1974, but it was shuttered again in 1983 because the vendor failed to maintain the facility. When the park sought a new operator, there were no bids.

After a successful fund-raising effort in the late 1980s, the Prospect Park Alliance hired Will Morton VIII, a Colorado-based sculptor and one of the few antique merry-go-round restorers in the United States, to refurbish the animals and chariots, battered after twenty-eight years of galloping for enchanted children. The Carousel's air-pumped Wurlitzer band organ was also restored, filling the park once again with the sounds and music of a bygone era.

The high-profile Carousel project confirmed the Alliance's ability to accomplish large projects. Foundations were now willing to provide substantial grants, and fund-raising efforts from private sources were bearing fruit. In 1989 the Alliance raised $777,005, and that amount nearly tripled to $2,088,056 in 1995. These added financial resources allowed the organization to provide some protection against economic downturns and helped offset parks-department budget cuts during the severe recession in the early 1990s.

The new administration continued to face the same challenges as previous management, but it also faced many new ones. Public use of the park increased significantly during the second half of the 1980s, after years of neglect. This surge in popularity was dubbed the "second assault." (The first assault was the devastation wrought by neglect in the 1960s and 1970s).[13] By the early 1990s, 6 million annual visitors were coming to the park, in contrast to 1.7 million just one

The park's first Carousel was located in the Rose Garden.

ABOVE
Today's restored Carousel is
a delight for children and also
attracts adults, who discover
their inner child.

RIGHT
Generations of families
have experienced the
Carousel's magic.

decade earlier. They pounded the turf, wandered through the woods, and wore out facilities in public buildings—maintenance and sustainability became even more crucial. Stranahan had stressed the importance of maintaining the park a century earlier, but keeping up the landscape and buildings was but one challenge among several. Community outreach was equally important, as were environmental education and expansion of the ranks of volunteers to foster a sense of stewardship so that the park would never again be neglected.

Landscape Restoration

Buildings came first in the restoration of Prospect Park, but the landscape was not ignored. In 1980 the parks department hired consultants to develop historic landscape studies for three areas— the Ravine, the Long Meadow, and Grace Hill—with the eventual aim of their restoration. Two years later, similar studies were completed for the Lake and the park perimeter. The Landscape Management Office, formed in 1988, and the 1994 Landscape Management Plan served to codify the newfound emphasis on landscape in the park's restoration. This followed the establishment of a ten-person horticultural crew in 1981 to maintain the park's woodlands and meadows—the first time in twenty years that Prospect Park had a gardening staff. The crew planted and pruned trees, maintained the many areas of turf, fertilized the grounds, and cared for the perimeter plantings.

Actual landscape restoration was first implemented in the park in the mid-1980s with the reconstruction of the ball fields at the Long Meadow's south end. Originally built under Moses in 1959 as temporary replacements while the Parade Ground fields were improved, the five diamonds were surrounded by a high, galvanized fence, obstructing access to the Long Meadow, and hulking brick bleachers, which destroyed the ninety-year-old view up the meadow. The undulating ice-age terrain so carefully groomed by Olmsted and Vaux was also flattened.

The fall beauty of the Ravine makes it hard to remember what it looked like twenty years ago.

While Olmsted had yet to achieve iconic status in the early 1980s, he had a loyal band of followers who wanted the ball fields removed completely and the Long Meadow returned to its original design. The athletic facilities were too popular with visitors, however. Park leaders eventually decided to construct two additional ball fields, bringing the total to seven, but all of them rebuilt closer to the meadow's edge. The bleachers and galvanized screening were removed and less-obtrusive black-vinyl-coated fencing that blended with the surrounding trees installed. When the ball fields reopened in 1984, Olmsted and Vaux's original vista through the meadow was restored.

A more comprehensive landscape project was the Prospect Park woodlands, encompassing 250 acres of woods and adjacent areas running through the park's center, from the Vale of Cashmere to Lookout Hill and including the Ravine. Once dense with trees and with a lush understory, by the 1980s the woodlands were suffering. The soil had been compacted by millions of walkers, birders, and mountain bikers, and no longer retained water or nutrients. The hard, bare earth repelled seeds, and the runoff washed soil and forest debris down gullied hillsides into the choked waterway. Trees and plantings, deprived of oxygen, could not adequately root themselves in the densely packed soil. The roots died along with the understory, and seemingly healthy but weakened trees toppled during windstorms. Many trees were invasive varieties, such as paper mulberry and Norway and sycamore maples, which crowded native trees, absorbed all the nutrients, and created dense canopies that restricted light, compounding the destruction. Ambergill, the meandering brook so carefully designed and made by Olmsted and Vaux, became a trickle—its shoreline denuded of vegetation—while Ambergill Falls had disappeared completely under a blanket of silt and rubble. One area was even used to deposit park garbage and debris. According to the Landscape Management Plan, "These last remaining woodlands in Brooklyn are faced with extinction if action is not taken soon.... A tour by even the most casual observer would reveal a horrible scene of neglect and decay."[14] Restoration of this area was slated to begin in 1988 but was postponed when funding was not available. Then, in 1991, the park received a substantial grant from the Lila Wallace-Reader's Digest Fund and established the Natural Resources Crew (NRC), whose task was to ensure the continual maintenance of Brooklyn's only forest.

The establishment of the NRC, under the Landscape Management Office, was crucial for the plan's implementation, because a sizable crew was necessary to maintain the natural areas over the twenty-five-year period allotted for their restoration. NRC staff mapped zones of erosion, bare soil, large colonies of invasive plants, and light gaps, and studied the distressed-forest areas to determine what kinds of trees and plants would be most suitable for the forest floor, understory, and canopy. On twenty-six plots in denuded sections of the park, staff members tested restoration strategies. They also grew trees, shrubs, and woody and herbaceous plants in a temporary greenhouse, experimenting with how best to grow various native-plant species from seeds.

A central question in the restoration planning was whether to reintroduce the same varieties of non-native ornamental plants that Olmsted and Vaux had selected when designing the park. It was the custom in the nineteenth century to use Asian and European plants to add color and texture to the landscape, but these exotics did not attract the bird and insect life essential to the park's ecology. In addition, the animals and diseases that would regulate the foreign plants in their native environments did not exist in Brooklyn. Exotics had been planted in a carefully manicured way that required dozens of horticulturists to maintain. Ed Toth, the first director of the Landscape Management Office, chose to use environmentally appropriate native plants that needed less care, fertilizer, and water than the plants specified by Olmsted and Vaux. The park turned to the Staten Island Native Plant Center (now the Greenbelt Native Plant Center) to propagate the hundreds of thousands of new plants and trees grown from seeds collected from around the region.

The work of the NRC crew was arduous. To deal with compaction, staff members and volunteers had to loosen the existing earth and add new top soil and compost, which was anchored by logs (water bars) and slowly decomposing jute netting to stabilize the ground and halt erosion. A ground cover including wildflowers was laid, and native woody plants and saplings were added to create root systems.

The Ambergill stream is hardly recognizable in this photo from the 1970s.

Restoring an incline section of landscape sometimes requires a layer of erosion-control fabric.

Restoration of the playgrounds was one of the first priorities for the surrounding neighborhoods. Imagination Playground now includes a water-splashing dragon that can also be climbed on.

Christian Zimmerman relied on an old photograph from 1885 (top) to pick the site for these new, small sugar maples (bottom).

Dead and dying trees were felled and left on the ground when it was feasible in order to return biomass to the site and provide habitat.

The capital restoration of the natural areas in the Ravine was overseen by the Design and Construction team, which was formed in 1987 to ensure that any renovation within the park—of buildings or landscape—met the needs of the people using the park, while maintaining Olmsted and Vaux's original, sweeping design. The initial staff of the team included Mary Fox, project manager of the Carousel restoration, landscape architect Rex Wassermann, and landscape designer Christian Zimmerman. A North Dakotan, Zimmerman has a deep and unusual understanding of landscape design, holding degrees in both horticulture and landscape architecture. These skills are most importantly put to use in his capacity now as vice president for Design and Construction, adapting Olmsted and Vaux's vision for modern use.

The team's earliest project was the 1989 reconstruction of the Vanderbilt Playground near Vanderbilt Street and Prospect Park West. Originally, the Vale of Cashmere and Rose Garden were the only areas in the park designed for children's play. It was not until the early twentieth century that more playgrounds were added. The park today maintains seven play areas, built along the perimeter to serve their respective neighborhoods.

The first major project for Design and Construction was the Ravine restoration, which began in 1996. It was by far the largest component of the overall natural-areas-restoration agenda and is considered by many to symbolize the turnaround of the park. It was not an easy task. The original construction plans for Prospect Park by Olmsted and Vaux were lost, and it was difficult to divine what plantings were used when the park was built or what their complete design intention was. Without the plans, the Design and Construction staff had to reconstruct the park's appearance by drawing information from letters, the few documents that remained from that era, and historical photographs.

The team conducted extensive research at the Library of Congress in Washington, D.C., and at Fairsted, Olmsted's home and office, now the Frederick Law Olmsted National Historic Site in Brookline, Massachusetts. They pored over documents, letters, photographs, and notes to gather detailed information about what was actually built and what was not, the designers' intent, and their overall philosophy. Additional sources included Louis Harmon Peet's 1902 book *Trees and Shrubs of Prospect Park*, which cataloged trees and their locations and helped the staff to determine which ones existed in the 1870s. They also reviewed archival documents from the 1930s that detailed the calipers of existing trees as well as topographical maps from the Moses administration. Design and Construction's research focus was determining what layers were added after Olmsted's and Vaux's departure—they examined annual modifications and, more significantly, the changes made during the City Beautiful movement and the Moses era.

The five-year Ravine restoration, begun with an initial $4.5 million allocation from Golden, had additional challenges. The undertaking

was as much an exercise in landscape archeology as landscape reconstruction. Zimmerman, aided by Dennis Madge, construction superintendent on the first segment of the restoration, was meticulous in preserving the Ravine's original design and restored it with an eye to details as minute as the correct height of a newly uncovered weir or the sound of water spilling over rocks.

The Ravine's man-made watercourse begins at the Upper Falls at the Fallkill and descends more than seventy feet on a sometimes shallow, sometimes steep grade to the Lake. By the 1980s, the once boisterous stream had become a trickle and was strewn with fallen boulders. The reconstruction began at the Fallkill waterfall, where the boulders were retrieved, numbered, and carefully hoisted into place—old photographs were used as references for positioning. In addition workers transported large boulders from a building site at the Methodist Hospital in Park Slope to replace ones that were missing. The restoration continued downstream at the Upper Pool, which was filled with decades of silt and lined by phragmites. It had not been dredged since 1915.

Before the renovation began, the pool's water flow was diverted around construction areas through large hoses to keep it flowing to the Lake and to save the existing aquatic life. Sunfish, crappies, pumpkin seeds, bass, and turtles were removed, placed in containers, and

These American elms were not in the original Olmsted and Vaux plan and therefore will live out their lives but will not be replaced.

The restored
Upper Falls at the Fallkill

The boulders of Rock Arch
Bridge in this early photo of the
1890s helped Zimmerman site the
reconstructed Ambergill Falls.

trucked to the Lake. The more the crews dug, the more silt and debris they encountered. An enormous amount of effort went into reversing the ravages of erosion and to further preventing silt from washing into the waterway. The erosion was caused, in part, by improper land management, but it was also a result of the ineffectiveness of the original engineering design. The pitch of the slope between two paths around Ambergill Falls was too steep and caused severe erosion. As a result, much of the runoff filled the Ambergill pool and obliterated Ambergill Falls.

Uncovering Ambergill Falls was a process similar to the search for the tomb of a lost pharaoh. Today we take the Ambergill's beauty for granted with its splashing, tumbling waters, the gladelike pools, and the high, lush hillsides. When the restoration began, however, the sides were bare, the stream was a mere thread of water, and there was no evidence of the falls. There were myths, tales, and daguerreotype-like photos, but no Ambergill Falls.

"We were tearing our hair out trying to find this waterfall," Zimmerman recalled. The staff was sure it existed, but where? No one knew until Toth found it serendipitously while walking on a path in the Ravine. He had paused to admire an artist sketching the landscape, when he noticed that the work included two foreground boulders similar to ones he had seen in an early photograph of the waterfalls. Toth hurried back to his office and retrieved a nineteenth-century photograph of the same boulders with Ambergill Falls in the background.

Toth and Zimmerman later realized that he had been standing on the capstone of the Rock Arch Bridge, under which water had once

run downstream to the Lake after it flowed down the falls. When the falls had collapsed, the watercourse was covered by silt, which had also filled in under the arch. Over time, the stream had worked its way around the arch, and a small wooden bridge with pipe railings was constructed over the new tributary. During the restoration, workers exposed the original bridge, which had been masterfully fashioned by nineteenth-century stonemasons.

Once the site of the Ambergill was discovered, the falls were painstakingly reconstructed, the pool excavated, and its surrounding embankments reinforced with modern construction blocks. Ambergill Falls slowly emerged as the magnificent, man-made depiction of nature as imagined and built by Olmsted and Vaux. The hillsides framing the falls were rebuilt using modern drainage techniques and then covered to create a natural appearance. When completed, these areas were fenced off to prevent visitors from wandering up and down the slopes and damaging the understory and causing erosion. The fencing was to be temporary, but it is now a permanent fixture to help preserve the Ravine and the surrounding woodlands. Olmsted and Vaux had suggested "barriers" in their time to protect the landscape from

LEFT
Ambergill Falls is completely man-made and has been restored to its original beauty.

RIGHT
Boulders were numbered to aid relocation.

OVERLEAF
A winter view of the winding Ambergill

The watercourse restoration extended to the Lullwater and the Binnen Falls. The triangular stone, called a sentinel, is a signature element in Olmsted designs and centers one's focus as it disperses the water.

Binnen Falls in the 1990s before it was restored

constant wear, but those were never installed.[15] Further downstream, the Ravine-restoration team tackled the Binnen and the Lily Pond Pools. Silt from erosion had turned the once expansive Binnen Pool into a meadow, graced by a fifty-five-foot-tall Himalayan pine in the center and traversed by a shallow rivulet. Work crews restored the original boundaries of the pool using old photographs as guides. The pine was removed by a payloader, its root ball carefully wrapped. The tree was then hoisted by crane to the pool's edge, where it was planted and where it still stands today.

The Music Grove Bridge, which crosses over the watercourse near the Music Pagoda, was rebuilt in its original rustic style but reinforced with steel I-beams to carry the load of modern trucks. Madge, an accomplished woodworker, reconstructed several other bridges and shelters in the park, basing his designs on old photographs of these structures. He scoured the woods near his home in upstate New York for the right cedars and tamaracks to fashion by hand and then transport to the park, where he assembled them with pegs and dowels.

The Ravine and pool restorations incorporated subtle and important changes to Olmsted and Vaux's design that met both aesthetic concerns and modern ecological needs. The park's stream and pools, dug to a depth of three to four feet, were originally created exclusively for aesthetic purposes without environmental concerns. By the late 1990s, however, park managers were conscious of the importance of

Fall accentuates the beauty
of the Lullwater as it winds its way
from the Boathouse to the Lake.

wildlife habitats. Native plants were sown along stream banks, and aquatic varieties were planted underwater at different depths to build a healthy ecosystem. The restored Binnen Pool was dug to a depth of nine feet, making it cool and suitable for frogs, turtles, and cold-blooded reptiles. The Lily Pond Pool was excavated, and a center island created to encourage nesting ducks and attract other birds.

The restoration extended beyond the Lily Pond to the Lullwater, which was drained and excavated. The aquatic life in this beautiful and gently curving waterway, which included two-foot-long bass, was transferred to the Lake, before front-end loaders dug out the phragmites and years of silt. The Brooklyn Bird Club offered advice on plants that are bird- and insect-friendly and that would have an invigorating effect on the park's environment. The area now has a healthy balance of birds, bats, and insects, including butterflies and dragonflies. The park's fifty species of butterflies are important for pollination, while some twenty-five types of dragonflies help eradicate mosquitoes. The number of bats in the park has doubled since the restoration.

The watercourse, with its increased stream flow, also attracts numerous species of birds. Before reconstruction, the stream was stagnant, filled with algae and bacteria, and the absence of bushes and shrubbery along its banks offered no protection from predators. Common breeds of migrating birds, such as the Baltimore oriole,

Lotus blossoms are reflected in
the Lily Pond, a wildlife habitat that
a short time ago was a swamp.

PREVIOUS
The restored Upper Pool
with a view of the Long Meadow
beyond the Dog Beach.

RIGHT
The Midwood, now heavily forested,
is a favorite site for birders.

BELOW
A silhouetted blue heron
stalks in the marshland of the Lake.

increased significantly after the restoration, along with the warbling vireo and the blue-gray gnatcatcher. There is great excitement among bird-watchers when rare species are sighted, such as the orange-crowned or prothonotary warbler.

Prospect Park is in fact a strategic point at the convergence of the New England and Atlantic flyways, the migration corridors used by birds to fly to and from the Arctic Circle and Newfoundland. Migrating species travel from southern climates in the United States and South America and use the long ridge of the park's terminal moraine as a navigational aid. In the fall and spring the park is an oasis of green and provides birds with a vital resting area and feeding ground. It is not unusual during these migratory periods to spot as many as seventy-five to one hundred different bird species in one day, including the bald eagles that follow the ridge with the northwest winds in September. Some birds winter in the park while others alight for only a short time—like the blackpoll warbler, on its way to

Argentina from Hudson Bay, or the ruby-throated hummingbird, traveling from the Berkshires across the Gulf of Mexico to the Yucatan Peninsula.

Keeping track of bird populations is an important activity in Prospect Park. The Brooklyn Bird Club and the Audubon Center sponsor an annual bird count; more than two hundred species have been reported in the park. Independent ornithologists track birds by snaring them in mist nets, weighing and tagging them, and taking blood samples before releasing them. One purpose of the research is to determine if the park's plant life provides adequate nutrition for long migratory flights.[16]

New Building Projects

Concurrent with the woodlands project were other renovations in the park, including work on McKim, Mead & White's Grand Army Plaza entrance. The restoration focused on refurbishing the battered yellow pavers, the four bronze eagles, the deteriorating pavilions and guardhouse, and the snake-handled urns.

The Prospect Park Zoo also underwent reconstruction—a five-year, $37 million project, starting in 1988. Before being refurbished, the zoo had had a reputation for being one of the ten worst in the country. The animal care was poor; the facility lacked funding and was plagued by vandalism; and litter abounded. In 1987 an eleven-year-old boy was killed by polar bears when he scaled the fences and crossed the moat of their compound. The exteriors of the Aymar Embury II–designed buildings were preserved, but the dilapidated interiors were gutted and the animal pits and cages demolished. Reopened in 1993, the zoo is now operated and maintained by the Wildlife Conservation Society, which also runs the Bronx and Central Park Zoos as well as the New York Aquarium. In keeping with its objective of teaching children about animals and their natural surroundings, the zoo now includes classrooms in its Discovery Center and offers interactive exhibits for children, all funded by the parks department.

Another important restoration project was the Boathouse, which was renovated, for the third time in thirty years, beginning in 1997 with a $5 million capital project funded by the city. In 1971 the Boathouse became the park's first large-scale preservation project when its red-tiled roof was replaced and the original, hand-carved terra-cotta facade restored. In 1984 the interior was restored, and the exterior repainted and sealed. Early Boathouse architectural drawings show an open building, without doors and designed for warm weather use. Doors were added later, but the lack of heat in the building guaranteed that there would be problems. By the 1990s the roof leaked; the 1971 restored terra-cotta was falling off; and the glazed surfaces were peeling. Park employees entering the Boathouse were sometimes greeted with water on the floor and icicles hanging from the ceiling.

Relying on architectural drawings and photographs from the archives of Columbia University and the park, the Design and Construction team, led by park architect Ralph Carmosino, started a thorough reconstruction. Sixty percent of the exterior terra-cotta

facade from the 1971 restoration was replaced with a new, thicker one. The 1971 terra-cotta had been machine-manufactured and was only three-quarters of an inch thick—compared to what originally was four inches—and cracked during the freeze-thaw cycle. Back then little was known about how to maintain terra-cotta. The new restoration team, by contrast, drew on knowledge gained during the restoration of Manhattan's Woolworth Building in the late 1980s and constructed a cavity wall behind the facade with flashing and weeps (vents) to allow for proper drainage and installed a heating system to prevent moisture buildup in the walls.

The ceiling of the Boathouse is covered by iridescent green Guastavino tiles arranged in herringbone patterns on crisscrossing vaulted arches. Damaged ceiling tiles were replaced, and on the terrace replicas of the original dolphin-themed lamp standards were installed. Yellow brick pavers on the front terrace replaced the red ones that had been laid during a previous restoration. The design team surmised that architect Frank J. Helmle had used yellow pavers when the Boathouse was built in 1905, and their hunch proved correct when later excavations revealed the original bricks.

A new dock was constructed for the thirty-foot electric boat that tours the Lake. Named *Independence*, it is a fiberglass reproduction of the park's late nineteenth-century boat of the same name that remained in service into the 1930s. Both the current and the original boats were built by the Electric Launch Company, which introduced electric-motor boats at the World's Columbian Exposition in 1893. The company's boats would replace gasoline-powered vessels, which were nicknamed "explosive boats" because they frequently caught fire or exploded.

Educational Outreach

As important as the Boathouse restoration was, its adaptive reuse as the Prospect Park Audubon Center was equally significant. National Audubon had originally proposed to build a fifty-acre education center in 1966, located at the Upper Pool with grounds that would extend to Ambergill Falls, but the plan was rejected by Park Commissioner August Heckscher as being too intrusive. In 2002 the newly renovated Boathouse reopened as National Audubon's first urban nature center. The Prospect Park Alliance had found an ideal partner in Audubon with whom to educate the public about local ecology and the environment in general. The center is operated by the Alliance, while Audubon New York provides a portion of the funding and some staff training. Nearly one hundred thousand visitors—including thousands of students—annually take part in Audubon Center programs and activities about the environment and wildlife.

Children can crawl through exhibits that include a larger-than-life oriole nest, discover how birds see, learn from a naturalist how to differentiate between species, and take nature walks through the park. There are lectures using live birds of prey during Hawk Weekend, and tours at dusk as bats begin their nightly forays. Birding walks are offered year-round and attract a hearty following, as do summer wine-and-cheese gatherings that close with a moonlit electric-boat ride on the Lullwater and the Lake.

The Lefferts Historic House Museum forms another important component of the park's educational outreach, containing more than two hundred years of Brooklyn history. Five generations of the Lefferts family occupied the homestead on land granted by Peter Stuyvesant in 1661. The original building, located in what was then

The great egret, here in its breeding plumes, is often seen near the Boathouse.

The Lefferts House, built just after the American Revolution, was moved four blocks to the park and is now an educational center. A replica of the Flatbush plank road runs behind the wagon.

the village of Flatbush, was destroyed by fire during the Battle of Brooklyn but was reconstructed shortly afterward. African slaves, indentured servants, and hired hands produced wheat, flax, hemp, and corn, and later potatoes, on the farm's 240 acres. After the Civil War, as the family business shifted from farming to commerce, the land was worked by tenant farmers and eventually was subdivided for housing. Donated to New York City by the estate of John Lefferts in 1918, the house was moved four blocks to Prospect Park. In 1920 it opened as a house museum and was, for more than seventy years, operated by the Daughters of the American Revolution. Today it is administered by the Prospect Park Alliance in conjunction with the Historic House Trust of New York City.

The Lefferts House is a typical early Dutch farmhouse—one of fourteen surviving in Brooklyn—with a gambrel roof and a deep porch. Park educators offer tours of the parlor and an upstairs bedroom that depict daily life in the 1820s. Brooklyn children work the garden soil with their hands and learn to understand the ecological importance of planting rye in the fall as a cover crop to provide nutrients for spring potatoes. They pump water by hand and bake bread in an outdoor brick oven, all the while learning the ways of Native Americans, slaves, and the early Dutch settlers during a time when most food was grown locally.[17]

The Parade Ground and the Drives

Education is an important component of the Alliance's outreach, but as it enters the twenty-first century, so too are athletics. On the Parade Ground hundreds of contests are in full swing during spring, summer, or fall: Pee Wee baseball, Hispanic women's soccer, and football are all underway simultaneously on this forty-acre plot, where militia groups once paraded. On the northeast corner is the Tennis Center, rebuilt in 2006, which includes eleven composite courts enclosed during winter and a patio for social gatherings.

For years the Parade Ground was a Brooklyn institution as well-known as the Dodgers's Ebbets Field. Many baseball stars developed their skills on the ground's ball fields. Eighteen-year-olds signed contracts on the sidewalk, while scouts hovered about to discover the likes of Sandy Koufax, who was pitching for the Coney Island Parkviews. Later players included the famed John Candeleria, Joe Peppitone, and Lee Mazzilli. From the 1920s to the 1950s, organized leagues at the Parade Ground played to crowds that often reached twenty thousand on weekend afternoons.

The Parade Ground was partially restored in 1982, but it again deteriorated because of inadequate maintenance. By 2000 all of the athletic fields were either swamps or dust bowls filled with potholes. The new Parade Ground, completed in 2004, has eleven reconstructed athletic fields, including baseball, softball, football, soccer, and multipurpose fields, as well as basketball and volleyball courts and full-service concessions facilities with picnic and seating areas. Six of the fields, equipped with artificial turf, can be used year-round.

Among the other venues for vigorous physical activity in the park are its drives. While Olmsted and Vaux designed them for more passive, leisurely carriage riding, they are today the most-used recreational space in Prospect Park. Once the automobile was introduced in the early twentieth century, the drives became noisy thoroughfares disconnected from the ambience of the park. By the mid-twentieth century, the drives provided an easier, faster commute from one part

of the city to another. Neighborhood groups applauded them because they reduced local traffic, and the police approved because they believed that greater number of cars in the park would mean more people and increased safety. But instead of keeping the city at bay, the drives brought the city into the park. For motorists, the park's beauty was secondary to reaching their destinations quickly, while for park visitors, the cars were just additional urban obstacles. Today the drives are only open to cars during weekday rush hours, which creates wonderful opportunities for thousands of runners, walkers, skateboarders, and bicyclists.

The Future of the Park

Over the years the Alliance has evolved from an entrepreneurial start-up to an established organization, and with its help Prospect Park has risen from the ashes. Most buildings and much of the landscape and the cherished views have been restored. The park is now a major destination for millions of visitors each year—nearly ten million in 2010—and it has become a venue for a variety of festivals and events.

In 2011 the Alliance embarked on its most ambitious project ever with the construction of the $74 million Lakeside, a multiuse facility to replace Wollman Rink. The project also re-creates Music Island along with the charming Tear Drop Island and adds five acres to the Lake as well as three acres of green space along the shoreline at the foot of the Concert Grove. Designed by architects Tod Williams and Billie Tsien with Zimmerman as landscape architect and project manager, this facility will fit seamlessly into the park's fabric and qualify for LEED certification. Backed into a man-made hillside with a grass-covered roof, the building will blend with its surroundings. The demolition of Wollman Rink and the reappearance of Music Island as a wildlife refuge after fifty years will enable the public to once again enjoy unobstructed and magnificent vistas across the Lake.

Responding to community needs, the designers of Lakeside included two skating rinks—one under cover for ice hockey and special events, and one in the open for free-form skating. The rinks can be used year-round and are adaptable in the summers for roller-skating and water activities. Lakeside is also a community center for educational and recreational events and houses a cafe and a seating area that will partly complete Olmsted and Vaux's plan for a terraced lakeside restaurant—the Refectory. Perhaps most significant, however, is that Lakeside will once again fulfill the original designers' desire for the area around the Concert Grove to become a major focal point, drawing visitors through the park to the Lake. Included in the project is a rebuilt portion of the 1870 Promenade, paved and bordered with bluestone, which will meander from Music Island to the rustic shelter beyond Duck Island.

Lakeside is funded by a mixture of government sources and private donations, including $10 million from the Leon Levy Foundation, the largest donation in the park's history. This structure of private and public support has allowed the Alliance to continue to serve as a critical buffer between the park and the never-ending

The restored Tear Drop Island

disruptions—from devastating natural disasters to crippling economic recessions. The Lakeside project, thanks to this support, will lead Prospect Park into the new century with its state-of-the-art design, just as the City Beautiful movement ushered it into the twentieth century. The scale of the project also symbolizes the current appreciation of parks, which are seen—more than ever—as vital to urban life. Cities, using significantly less energy per capita than rural areas, are said to be the future in this era of global warming. New York City is expected to gain one million more residents by 2030, and Mayor Michael Bloomberg's administration is developing plans to place a park within a ten-minute walk of every resident—whether they are small playgrounds and neighborhood lots or repurposed riverfront piers, such as the Brooklyn Bridge Park, retired military bases, abandoned rail lines, or former landfills.

Brooklynites repeatedly state they stay in their borough because of Prospect Park—not only because of its natural beauty in a dense urban area but, as Olmsted and Vaux realized 150 years ago, because of its emotional and physical benefits. For the young, it is a place to play and understand the environment. As people age it becomes a vital antidote to such afflictions as obesity and high blood pressure. Even a regular twenty-minute stroll through the park can help improve one's health significantly.

Parks are more than just the lungs of a city; they are its soul and spirit. To this day, the Long Meadow is a mosaic of Brooklyn's diversity, with games of soccer, touch football, rugby, Irish hurling, and Caribbean cricket going on cheek by jowl. Park visitors picnic, fly kites, celebrate birthdays, or stroll on the paths. The Parade Ground is a sports festival. The drives are alive, and Grand Army Plaza becomes a bustling green market on weekends. Crowds come to see the New York Philharmonic perform in the park or to pay homage

RIGHT
It is hard to leave the
park on a beautiful spring night.

OPPOSITE
A park visitor exercises under
a flowering magnolia tree.

to Michael Jackson sponsored by Spike Lee. With elaborate barbecuing apparatuses, they stake out spots in the Picnic Ground to eat, play, rest, and doze.

While the Alliance focuses on the park's present, it also looks to the future. Lakeside is not the end of efforts to restore Prospect Park. There are numerous capital projects that will take years to complete, and once they are, it will undoubtedly be time to start the restoration process over again. Some of the future projects include the restoration of the Concert Grove and the Oriental Pavilion along with the entire area north of the zoo along Flatbush Avenue, through the Vale of Cashmere to Grand Army Plaza. There is talk about turning the vale back into a playground and creating more opportunities for education around important sites from the Battle of Brooklyn and the Revolutionary War. The paths around the Lake will need rebuilding—many show signs of erosion.

Prospect Park is a living work of art requiring continual nurturing, and the elements are in place now to sustain it into the future. The Prospect Park Alliance, the New York City Parks and Recreation Department, Brooklyn officials, and the plethora of local volunteers and community organizations that have always been central to the park's development are committed to ensuring that Prospect Park continues to thrive. When Thomas and Christensen retired, the baton was passed to a new board chair, Albert Garner, and a new president and administrator, Emily Lloyd. Both are intent on respecting the park's original design and social philosophy in their efforts to manage and sustain it. Olmsted and Vaux designed Prospect Park for future generations, not only for the city but also, as they said, for people of the world. The park has endured for more than 150 years and remains true to its ideal: it serves as an exquisite public space that is a celebration of diversity and welcoming to all. It is vibrant. It is life affirming. It is a masterpiece.

Notes

Introduction

1 The term "pleasure ground" was used frequently in the mid-nineteenth century to describe what we today call a public park.

2 Allan Nevins and Milton Halsey Thomas, eds., *The Diary of George Templeton Strong: Post-War Years 1865–75* (New York: MacMillan, 1952), 374.

3 Frederick Law Olmsted and Calvert Vaux, *Preliminary Report to the Commissioners for Laying Out a Park in Brooklyn, New York* (Olmsted, Vaux & Co., Landscape Architects, January 24, 1866). In Charles E. Beveridge and Carolyn F. Hoffman, eds., *The Papers of Frederick Law Olmsted: Writings on Public Parks, Parkways, and Park Systems*, supplementary series, vol. I, (Baltimore: Johns Hopkins University Press, 1997), 93.

Chapter 1

1 Natalie A. Naylor, *Journeys on Old Long Island* (Interlaken, NY: Empire State Books, 2002), Review by Janet Gruner, 3.

2 John J. Gallagher, *The Battle of Brooklyn 1776* (New York: Sarpedon, 1995), 116.

3 *Twenty-seventh Annual Report of the Department of Parks for the Year 1887*, Brooklyn, 30.

4 Henry Reed Stiles, *The History of the City of Brooklyn* (Brooklyn, NY: Subscription, 1867–70), 208.

5 David Boroff, "Beach, Bohemia, Barracks— Brooklyn," *New York Times*, September 29, 1963, 233.

6 Stiles, *The History of the City of Brooklyn*, 254.

7 Ibid, 271.

8 Ibid, 290.

9 Edwin G. Burrows and Mike Wallace, *Gotham, A History of New York to 1898* (New York: Oxford University Press, 1999), 450.

10 Kenneth T. Jackson and David S. Dunbar, *Empire City: New York Through the Centuries* (New York: Columbia University Press, 2002), 238.

11 "Brooklyn Association for Improving the Condition of the Poor," *New York Times*, October 28, 1857, 8.

12 "Washington Park," *Brooklyn Daily Eagle*, June 15, 1846, 2.

13 "Pure Air and Play," *Brooklyn Daily Eagle*, June 11, 1847, 2.

14 "The Commissions," *Brooklyn Daily Eagle*, January 27, 1873, 4.

15 Roy Rosenzweig and Elizabeth Blackmar, *The Park and the People, A History of Central Park* (Ithica and London: Cornell University Press, 1992), 191.

16 "The Commissions," *Brooklyn Daily Eagle*, January 27, 1873, 4.

17 "Prospect Park," Report of Egbert L. Viele, Esq., to the Commissioners for the Improvement of Prospect Park, Brooklyn, January 15, 1861, 25, Prospect Park Archives.

18 Ibid, 27.

19 Ibid, 25.

20 "Views of Correspondents," *Brooklyn Daily Eagle*, May 21, 1860, 2.

21 Ibid.

22 "Arguments of Commissioner Stranahan," *Brooklyn Daily Eagle*, March 31, 1869, 1.

23 "Prospect Park: How It Looked When the Commissioners Took Charge of It," *Brooklyn Daily Eagle*, June 29, 1891, 3.

24 "Changes of a Decade," *Brooklyn Daily Eagle*, July 19, 1870, 2.

25 Ibid.

Chapter Two

1 James S. T. Stranahan, *An Account of the Dinner at the Hamilton Club to Honor James S. T. Stranahan December 13, 1888* (Brooklyn, NY: Hamilton Club, 1889).

2 "Prospect Park," *Brooklyn Daily Eagle* August 1, 1871, 3.

3 "Cost Figures for Prospect Park Construction," Papers of Charles Downing Lay, 1877–1956, Prospect Park Archives and "J. S. T. Stranahan," *Brooklyn Daily Eagle*, February 2, 1874, 4.

4 "The Park President, A Local Poet on the Case of Hunter Versus Stranahan," *Brooklyn Daily Eagle*, July 19, 1873, 2.

5 "The Mystery of the Great Magician," *Brooklyn Daily Eagle*, March 8, 1871, 2.

6 "Mayor Hunter, Mr. Stranahan and Prospect Park," *Brooklyn Daily Eagle*, February 6, 1874, 2.

7 "J. S. T. Stranahan 87 Years Old," *New York Times*, April 26, 1895, 1.

8 Interview with reporter, *Brooklyn Daily Eagle*, December 23, 1894, n.p.

9 "Walks About the City," *Brooklyn Daily Eagle*, June 18, 1886, n.p.

10 "Will Be There," *Brooklyn Daily Eagle*, June 5, 1891, 6.

11 Ibid.

12 "Brooklyn's Latest Enterprises," *Brooklyn Daily Eagle*, July 21, 1871, 3.

13 "The Park Magician," *Brooklyn Daily Eagle*, January 27, 1878, 4.

14 "Mr. Stranahan Dead," *Brooklyn Daily Eagle*, September 3, 1898, 1.

15 Ibid.

16 "The Stranahan Statue," *New York Times*, June 7, 1891, n.p.

17 "J. S. T. Stranahan Dead," *New York Times*, September 4, 1898, n.p.

18 "Dr. H. P. Dewey's Tribute to James S. T. Stranahan," *Brooklyn Daily Eagle*, October 13, 1902, 13.

19 Francis Kowsky, *Country, Park, & City: The Architecture and Life of Calvert Vaux* (New York: Oxford University Press, 1998), 8.

20 Ibid, 7.

21 Elizabeth Barlow, *Frederick Law Olmsted's New York* (New York: Praeger Publishers, 1972), 33.

22 Calvert Vaux, *Villas & Cottages* (New York: Harper & Brothers, 1857), 52.

23 Ibid.

24 Kowsky, *Country, Park, & City*, 26.

25 Ibid, 29.

26 Frederick Law Olmsted, *Walks and Talks of an American Farmer in England*, (1852, repr.; Amherst and Boston: Library of American Landscape History, 2002).

27 Kowsky, *Country, Park, & City*, 282.

28 Vaux, *Villas & Cottages*, 18.

29 Ibid, 56.

30 Audio tape for visitors to the Metropolitan Museum of Art, describing renovations to the second-floor gallery that uncovered portions of the original facade designed by Vaux, Metropolitan Museum of Art, New York.

31 Vaux designed a number of city parks, including the Canal Street Park, Jackson Square, Abingdon Square, Duane Street Park, Christopher Street Park, East River Park, Lincoln Square Park, Corlear's Hook Park, and Greeley Square. Kowsky, *Country, Park, & City*, 306–7.

32 Barlow, *Frederick Law Olmsted's New York*, 16.

33 Witold Rybczynski, *A Clearing in the Distance* (New York: Scribners, 1999), 261.

34 The Frederick Law Olmsted Papers project has produced, since 1981, seven volumes and one supplementary one, presenting the papers along with footnoted interpretations of Olmsted's work. Work continues on volumes VIII and IX and supplementary volumes II and III. The works are edited by Charles Capen McLaughlin, deceased, Charles E. Beveridge, and Carolyn F. Hoffman, and are published by the Johns Hopkins University Press under the title *The Papers of Frederick Law Olmsted: Writings on Public Parks, Parkways, and Park Systems*.

35 Rybczynski, *A Clearing in the Distance*, 39.

36 Nevins, Thomas, eds., *The Diary of George Templeton Strong*, 243.

37 Ibid, 291.

38 Melvin Kalfus, *Frederick Law Olmsted: The Passion of the Public Artist* (New York and London: New York University Press, 1990), 71.

39 Rybczynski, *A Clearing in the Distance*, 83.

40 Rybczynski, *A Clearing in the Distance*, 45.

41 Olmsted, *Walks and Talks of an American Farmer in England*, 91, 93.

42 Ibid, 147.

43 The *Horticulturist and Journal of Rural Art and Rural Taste* was Downing's magazine, which he published and edited from 1846 to 1852.

44 Lewis Mumford, *The Brown Decades: The Study of Arts in America, 1865–95* (New York: Dover, 1959), 38.

45 Rybczynski, *A Clearing in the Distance*, 165.

46 Ibid, 210.

Chapter Three

1 Olmsted and Vaux, *Preliminary Report to the Commissioners for Laying Out a Park in Brooklyn*, 91.

2 Rybczynski, *A Clearing in the Distance*, 180.

3 Olmsted, *Walks and Talks of an American Farmer in England*, 91.

4 Ibid, 91, 98.

5 Olmsted and Vaux, *Preliminary Report to the Commissioners for Laying Out a Park in Brooklyn*, 90.

6 Ibid, 87.

7 Daniel M. Bluestone, "From Promenade to Park: The Gregarious Origins of Brooklyn's Park Movement," *American Quarterly* 39, no. 4 (Winter 1987): 541.

8 *First Annual Report of the Brooklyn Park Commissioners*, Brooklyn, 1861.

9 "Prospect Park, The Drive," *Brooklyn Daily Eagle*, June 20, 1867, 2.

10 *Ninth Annual Report of the Brooklyn Park Commissioners*, Brooklyn, 1869, 337.

11 Olmsted, *Walks and Talks of an American Farmer in England*, 92.

12 "Prospect Park," *Brooklyn Daily Eagle*, August 1, 1871.

13 "Charles C. Martin Dead," *New York Times*, July 12, 1903.

14 Olmsted and Vaux, *Preliminary Report to the Commissioners for Laying Out a Park in Brooklyn*, 99.

15 "Prospect Park," *Brooklyn Daily Eagle*, August 1, 1871.

Chapter Four

1 Prospect Park, *Brooklyn Daily Eagle*, June 2, 1874, 4.

2 Beveridge et al., eds., *The Papers of Frederick Law Olmsted*, supplementary series, vol. I, 188.

3 Ibid, 519.

4 Ibid, 182.

5 "Seen In Prospect Park," *Brooklyn Daily Eagle*, June 17, 1888, 4.

6 "The Archery Tournament," *Harpers Weekly*, July 23, 1881, n.p.

7 "Seen in Prospect Park," *Brooklyn Daily Eagle*, June 17, 1888, 4.

8 "Age of Innocence, Early Letters from Edith Wharton," *New Yorker*, June 29, 2009, 35.

9 "Seen in Prospect Park," *Brooklyn Daily Eagle*, June 17, 1888, 4.

10 "Regattas in Miniature," *New York Times*, May 8, 1927, n.p.

11 "Skating in Prospect Park," *New York Times*, December 12, 1880, n.p.

12 Beveridge et al., eds., *The Papers of Frederick Law Olmsted*, supplementary series, vol. I, 188.

13 "Prospect Park Picnics," *Brooklyn Daily Eagle*, August 15, 1886, 11.

14 "The Lily Pond," *Civic News*, Prospect Park Archives, 10.

15 "Brower Begins A Crusade," *Brooklyn Daily Eagle*, May 1, 1893, 10.

16 "Prospect Park Picnics," *Brooklyn Daily Eagle*, August 15, 1886, 11.

17 Ibid.

18 Ibid.

19 *Twenty-Seventh Annual Report of the Department of Parks for the Year 1887*, Brooklyn, 5.

20 "Nellie's Tree," *Brooklyn Daily Eagle*, August 13, 1882, 6.

21 "The Lily Pond," *Civic News*, Prospect Park Archives, 10.

22 "The Coaching Parade," *Brooklyn Daily Eagle*, May 24, 1891, 20.

23 The prominent Brooklyn-based Congregationist clergyman, noted for his abolitionist stands, was accused of committing adultery with a member of his congregation. The sensational trial took place in 1875. Beecher was acquitted.

24 "At Prospect Park," *Brooklyn Daily Eagle*, May 22, 1881, 6.

25 "The Cricket Field," *New York Times*, July 3, 1877.

26 "Society," *New York Times*, September 13, 1896, n.p.

27 "Polo for the Astor Cup," *New York Times*, September 23, 1895, n.p.

28 "Minister Answers Mayor," *New York Times*, July 14, 1912, n.p.

29 "A Victim of the Bicycle," *New York Times*, October 20, 1880, n.p.

30 "The Wheelmen's Humble Plee," *New York Times*, April 18, 1887, n.p.

31 "Wheelmen on Parade," *New York Times*, September 13, 1885, n.p.

32 "Grand Parade of Cyclers," *New York Times*, June 21, 1891, 5.

33 Ibid.

34 Ibid.

35 "Chasing in the Moonlight," *New York Times*, April 8, 1887, 3.

36 "Prospect Park Errors," *Brooklyn Eagle*, July 8, 1888, 10.

37 Olmsted draft of a letter to Vaux (summer 1894), Prospect Park Archives.

38 Olmsted letter to Stranahan, in *The First Historic Landscape Report for the Ravine, Prospect Park*, Walmsley & Company, 1986, 72.

39 "Victoria Regia In Bloom," *Brooklyn Daily Eagle*, September 8, 1897, 5.

40 Ibid.

41 Ibid.

42 "Bad Bear Sent to Brooklyn," *New York Times*, May 11, 1902, n.p.

43 "Prospect Park," *Brooklyn Daily Eagle*, August 1, 1871, n.p.

44 Twelfth Annual Report of the Commissioners of Prospect Park for the Year 1871, 10.

45 *Twenty-Seventh Annual Report of the Department of Parks for the Year 1887*, Brooklyn, 17.

46 *Thirty-first and Thirty-second Annual Reports of the Department of Parks for the Years 1891 and 1892*, Brooklyn, n.p.

47 *Twenty-Eight Annual Report of the Department of Parks for the Year 1888*, n.p.

48 "Left to Rot in Prospect Park," *New York Times*, August 15, 1892, n.p.

49 "Park Work," *Brooklyn Daily Eagle*, August 18, 1886, n.p.

50 *Twenty-Seventh Annual Report of the Department of Parks for the Year 1887*, Brooklyn, 28.

51 "Brooklyn's New Electric Fountain," *Scientific American*, August 22, 1897.

52 "Ada Louise Huxtable, It Isn't Green Cheese," *New York Times*, May 21, 1972, 25.

53 Letter from Frederick Law Olmsted to Commissioner Frank Squier, June 25, 1895, Prospect Park Archives.

54 "Statues in Prospect Park," *Brooklyn Daily Eagle*, July 28, 1895, 24.

55 "Adorning Prospect Park," *Brooklyn Daily Eagle*, June 15, 1871, 4.

56. "Address to [the] Prospect Park Scientific Association," May 1868, Olmsted Papers, Library of Congress, 155.

57 "50,000 In Brooklyn Greet Bernhardt," *New York Times*, July 5, 1917, 3.

58 During the war there were several acres put aside in the park for vegetable gardens. These were called "victory gardens."

59 "Her point of View," *New York Times*, October 22, 1893.

60 "Santa Arrives in Airplane," *New York Times*, November 27, 1927, 2.

61 *Annual Report*, Department of Parks, Borough of Brooklyn, City of New York, 1926–1927, 39.

Chapter Five

1 Edward Koch (mayor of New York 1979–88), interview with author, February 26, 2008.

2 Joseph and Mary Merz (architects, Prospect Park curators in 1976), interview with author, July 24, 2009.

3 Ibid.

4 "Roosevelt Scored at Patriotic Fete," *New York Times*, April 27, 1936, n.p.

5 "13,000 Anti-Reds Rally in Brooklyn," *New York Times*, May 3, 1927, n.p.

6 Alexander Garvin (educator, urban planner), phone interview with author, November 19, 2009.

7 "Lewis Mumford, Menageries and Piers," *New Yorker*, October 12, 1935, 36.

8   "Noisy Sea Lion Banished to Brooklyn," *New York Times,* December 14, 1935, n.p.

9   "Moses Agrees Queens Should Have a Zoo But He Can't See How to Finance Project," *New York Times,* March 29, 1957, n.p.

10   Al Franquinha (attorney, Brooklyn resident), interview with author, March 4, 2008.

11   Nicholas Gage, "Gallo Family Gets It Smart," *Lakeland Florida Ledger,* July 29, 1975, n.p.

12   Robert Makla (attorney, Prospect Park volunteer/preservationist), interview with author, May 8, 2010.

13   Howard Golden (Brooklyn borough president 1977–2001), interview with author, March 25, 2008.

14   "Roughs in Prospect Park," *New York Times,* June 26, 1884, n.p.

15   Grace Lichtenstein, "Weisl Fears Deterioration of Trees in Prospect Park," *New York Times,* January 4, 1975, 23.

16   Betty Smith, *A Tree Grows in Brooklyn* (Philadelphia: Blakiston Company, 1943).

17   "Project Under Way to Recapture Faded Glory of Prospect Park," *New York World Telegram,* August 10, 1959, 1.

18   Jane Jacobs, *The Death and Life of Great American Cities* (New York: Vintage, 1961).

19   Ada Louise Huxtable, "On the Right Track," *New York Times,* November 28, 1994, n.p.

20   Western Union telegram, Lewis Mumford to Donald Simon, Prospect Park curator, December 18, 1964, Prospect Park Archives.

21   Marianne Moore, "The Camperdown Elm," *New Yorker,* September 23, 1967, 48.

22   Marianne Moore, letter to M. M. Graff, Prospect Park Archives.

23   *Mayoral Candidate John V. Lindsay, White Paper on Prospect Park,* 1965, Prospect Park Archives.

24   "New City Parks Chief; Thomas Pearsall Field Hoving," *New York Times,* December 2, 1965, n.p.

25   "Hoving to Name Curators to Beautify City Parks," *New York Times,* December 12, 1965.

26   Ibid.

27   Ralph Blumenthal, "Future of Parks Stirs Civic Clash," *New York Times,* January 28, 1966, n.p.

28   "Lindsay on Parks Letter to Editor," *New York Times,* November 1, 1969, opinion page.

29   Donald Simon (former Prospect Park curator), interview with the author, March 26, 2009.

30   "Bikers Way Eased in Prospect Park," *New York Times,* July 13, 1975, n.p.

31   Patti Hagan, "Every Prospect Pleases, and Only Man is Vile," *New York Times,* March 4, 1973, n.p.

32   Deirdre Carmody, "Where New Yorkers Go and Don't Go," *New York Times,* January 18, 1974, 1.

33   "Brooklyn Loses Marianne Moore," *New York Times,* January 20, 1966, n.p.

34   "Ford To City: Drop Dead," *New York Daily News,* October 30, 1975, 1.

35   Roy Rosenzweig and Elizabeth Blackmar, *The Park and the People: A History of Central Park* (Ithica, NY: Cornell Univerity Press, 1992), 502.

Chapter Six

1   In 1926 the Plaza was renamed Grand Army Plaza on the occasion of the sixtieth anniversary of the Grand Army of the Republic, a civil war veterans group.

2   Anna Quindlen, "For Prospect Park, $10 Million to Recapture What Was," *New York Times,* January 4, 1980, n.p.

3   Howard Golden (Brooklyn borough president 1977–2001), phone interview with author, October 12, 2009.

4   Quindlen, "For Prospect Park," *New York Times.*

5   Ibid.

6   Gordon Davis (commissioner, New York City Department of Parks and Recreation 1978–83), interview with author, January 17, 2008.

7   Ibid.

8   "Topic Before and After," *New York Times,* July 12, 1984, n.p.

9   Donald Simon, "A Plan For All Seasons: The Design of Brooklyn's Prospect Park," *Long Island Historical Journal 3* (Fall 1990) 131.

10   New York City Department of Planning, "Population: The Newest New Yorkers," www.nyc.gov/dcp.

11   The Alliance's Community Committee, Com Com, was created in 1996 as a means of involving the community in almost every aspect of the park. Including some fifty-five organizations and elected officials, it has helped develop events and services, with a special focus on underserved park users. Com Com meets nine times a year and discussions range from police protection to zoning to playgrounds to how to keep people from dumping hot barbecue coals at the base of trees.

12   Douglas Martin, "Restoring Some Magic To Brooklyn," *New York Times,* October 7, 1989, n.p.

13   Prospect Park Landscape Management Office, Andropogan Associates, *A Landscape Management Plan for The Natural Areas of Prospect Par*k, 7.

14   Ibid.

15   *Fourteenth Annual Report of the Brooklyn Park Commissioners,* January 1874, 26.

16   The restoration of the watercourse and the land around it cost over $12 million and was funded by city capital funds with a few small private grants. However, the Alliance now funds the NRC for the park to ensure that all the work that was done in the natural areas will continue to be maintained.

17   The Prospect Park Administration has reached beyond the park to create stewardship for the future. In 2003 the Alliance partnered with the Brooklyn Botanic Garden and the New York City Department of Education to establish the Brooklyn Academy of Science and the Environment (BASE). Located in the former Prospect Heights High School, BASE offers field study for select students in Prospect Park and the Brooklyn Botanic Garden to supplement classroom teaching about science, nature, and the environment. Prospect Heights High School had a graduation rate of 27 percent; BASE not only increased that to 77 percent, but also had an attendance rate of 90 percent. Students graduate with an understanding of the natural world and the vital importance of protecting it.

Image Credits

All images © Elizabeth Keegin Colley unless otherwise noted.

Pages 14–15: © Prospect Park Alliance
Pages 18–19: © Alex Garvin
Pages 30, 31, 37, 38, 40–41, 43, 48, 64–65, 76 left, 82, 83, 88 top and bottom, 89 top left, 90 left, 92 bottom, 93 top, 99, 100–101, 103 top, 104, 105, 108 top, 110, 113, 114, 116 left, 126 left, 135, 136–37, 142, 162, 164, 168, 173 right, 175 bottom, 176 middle, 179 right, 182 bottom: © Prospect Park Archives
Page 33: Collection of David P. Colley
Pages 35, 60–61, 76 right, 92 top, 94 top, 95, 103 bottom, 106, 109 bottom, 112, 117 top, 125, 127 left, 129, 132, 141, 143 top, 169 left, 171, 178 bottom: © Prospect Park Archives/Bob Levine Collection
Pages 50, 55, 63, 84: Courtesy of the United States Department of the Interior, National Park Service, Frederick Law Olmsted National Historic Site
Page 52: © The Metropolitan Museum of Art. Image source: Art Resource, NY
Page 80 left: © Prospect Park Archives/Herbert Mitchell Collection
Page 85 left: © Collection of the Brooklyn Historical Society
Page 108 bottom: Prospect Park Archives/Courtesy of Renee Garrett
Page 109 top: © Prospect Park Archives/ J. J. Levison Collection
Pages 116 right, 155, 175 top: © New York City Parks Photo Archive
Page 148: © Prospect Park Archives/ Cookie Lorenzo Collection
Page 196 top left: Prospect Park Alliance/Laura Evans
Page 196 top right and bottom: © dbox, Inc.

Index